MW00737794

GOOD WITH MONEY

GOOD WITH MONEY

Kerry Gold with John Lefebvre

A RICH GUY'S GUIDE TO GAINING EVERYTHING BY LOSING IT ALL

Figure.1

Vancouver / Berkeley

Copyright © 2020 by John Cullen Lefebvre

20 21 22 23 24   5 4 3 2 1

All rights are reserved and no part of this publication may be reproduced, stored in a retrieval system, or transmitted in any form or by any means, electronic, mechanic, photocopying, scanning, recording or otherwise, except as authorized with written permission by the publisher. Excerpts from this publication may be reproduced under licence from Access Copyright.

Cataloguing data are available from Library and Archives Canada

ISBN 978-1-77327-129-3 (hbk.)
ISBN 978-1-77327-130-9 (ebook)
ISBN 978-1-77327-131-6 (pdf)

Design by Naomi MacDougall
Kerry Gold photograph by Mike Elsinga
John Lefebvre photograph by Billie Woods
Editing by Tyee Bridge
Copy editing by Judy Phillips
Jacket illustrations and lettering by Ben Frey

Printed and bound in Canada by Friesens
Distributed internationally by Publishers Group West

Figure 1 Publishing Inc.
Vancouver BC Canada
www.figure1publishing.com

Contents

"A man who dies rich dies disgraced."

ANDREW CARNEGIE

ONE

Stumbling into Tech

I AM STANDING on a sloped, wide-open stretch of Salt Spring Island, overlooking a glorious West Coast vista of ocean and distant mountains. It is the peak of summer, and the sky is a domed cup of blue. Salt Spring is the largest of the Gulf Islands, and somewhere in the distance are islands Galiano, Mayne, and Pender. A few kilometres away is the invisible American border that zigzags through the ocean and separates the San Juan Islands, on the horizon to the southeast. I'm here so that John Lefebvre can show me around his guesthouse property, a small collection of buildings that sit on four acres. Called Stonehouse, it was his year-round passion project before he got arrested thirteen years ago.

Lefebvre is a bear of a man, big and tall with shaggy grey hair. Today he's wearing, as he often does, a casual blazer with a leather man purse over one shoulder. Everywhere there is something to take in, something lovely or remarkable to enquire about. There are arts and crafts furniture and vintage cars in mint condition and a recording studio and soaring post-and-beam construction and perfectly placed skylights—and that never-ending view. There's even a stone circle in the style of Stonehenge that stands in the adjacent field, the work of artist and mason Ron Crawford. Two long-haired girls, both islanders, sit cross-legged on the grass, eating lunch. Lefebvre waves at them, greets them by name. They wave back. They might work for him, but it's unclear. It's the hippie-spirited Salt Spring Island way: keep it casual, stress-free. Serenity now.

Lefebvre has poured about $9 million into Stonehouse, including the cost of the property and renovations. It sits on agricultural land, so there are limitations on what he can do with it, and as far as businesses go, it's been a losing proposition. There are only five large guest suites for rent, and although it's a five-star property that gets stellar reviews, there's only so much revenue the guesthouse can bring in each year. But you get the feeling it was never about that. The property doubles as his office space and playground. It is the place where he and his wife Hilary Watson got married a few years ago, with tables set for eighty guests, covered in linen and crystal, and a stage for the band and a dance floor. He oversaw every detail of the renovation and the decor with his own particular vision, incorporating so much artwork that it has the feel of a gallery. Two massive bronze sculptures of headless kimono-wearing figures bookend the main entrance, each big enough for a dozen children to climb over. There is the long worn-wood table in the open dining area, the same table where he sat with the FBI the morning of his arrest in one of his Malibu homes. The kitchen counter is an imported slab of orange onyx lit from below, a giant glowing gemstone. He offers anecdotes about how he picked out the tiles for the bathrooms, and the hanging art pieces in the lobby. Some details are painstaking to the point that nobody but Lefebvre might appreciate them, such as the tiny, square cast-iron bird motifs he has incorporated throughout the guest suites, in the mouldings and between tiles. When he sees the smiling woman who manages the place, he gives her one of his bear hugs.

In what he calls the "garage-mahal," which is really a sleek contemporary loft, there is floor-to-ceiling artwork covering the two-storey walls. Lefebvre buys art with what seems to be a hoarder's compulsion. He picks up a painting still wrapped in its brown paper and wonders what it is.

He unwraps it.

"Oh, that one."

He remembers the artist, a local woman named Hannah Stone, but he can't remember when he purchased it.

"Isn't it beautiful?" he says happily and places it back down.

Lefebvre is openly proud of Stonehouse, which is an airier version of his home a few kilometres away, but on the ocean. On another trip, he shows me that house too.

Perhaps because he's a big man, he likes things larger than life—the house has a ceiling as high as a cathedral. Huge bronze sculptures, busts of people, flank that entrance too, and the interior, which feels dark and gothic, is packed with art, as are the grounds that slope to the rocky beach. As we walk and talk, I am startled by a human-sized sculpture of a dark cloaked figure. He says it also startled a visitor of his, the Dalai Lama's brother, who stayed at a guesthouse on the property with his wife, the founder of the Tibetan Nuns Project. He counts the Dalai Lama among his acquaintances, and many other accomplished people who've done deeply interesting, thoughtful things.

Lefebvre has always had a cavalier relationship with money: he can take it or leave it, he says. Because he avoided tedious tasks or anything remotely resembling a grind, he also had an uneasy relationship with a law career, and all the long hours and weekends spent working that the profession often demands. And he didn't fit the mould of a lawyer at all. In other lawyers' company, he felt like an outsider. He enjoyed meeting with clients, but he saw the corporate culture that valued fancy cars and country club memberships as the antithesis of 1960s counterculture. He tried various ways of making his profession adapt to his lifestyle, including working in his own community-oriented law office, where he'd take on pretty much any case that walked through the door. The end result was a career that moved in starts and stops, seguing into unlikely ventures, such as his stint as the owner of a leather goods shop, and another as a musician busking for change from commuters on their way to their white-collar jobs. These diversions—impulses to flee, really—went on for many years. By the time he was in his late forties, in the 1990s, he was pulling in around $35,000 a year from various legal work his friends found him, about the equivalent of what a junior reporter was making at a community newspaper. He's always lived for the day, so he wouldn't have taken stock. But to the observer, he was a middle-aged man with two failed marriages, buried under a mountain of debt to friends and family, and living on the second floor of a three-storey rental building in Calgary's inner city Mission district, where he grew up. As a boy he'd had a paper route on the very same street. When his daughter came to stay with him, she'd take the bedroom and he'd sleep on a futon in the living room. He was grateful the neighbours didn't complain about his upright piano, which he played often. His social nights consisted of friends at his apartment and wine that came in big bottles. His mother had loaned him the down payment for a lease on a $17,000 Toyota RAV4 Crossover SUV, and when he drove to restaurants or bars to play a gig, he felt consoled when he pulled up in it. He might be playing for a few dollars, but he had that car.

For all these reasons, and several more, John Lefebvre was not on track to become a super-millionaire with assets of around $350 million U.S. by age fifty-three. And yet, to everyone's surprise, that's what he did.

I have agreed to write his book for him, to tell his story, so this is an authorized account, Lefebvre's version of his story as he's told it to me. Over the course of several months, we met up on the island, but also near his apartment on Vancouver's west side, at a favourite French café with marble-topped bar and tables. One day, sitting by an open window, a tall African woman walks by in a traditional twisted-up head wrap and long dress, an explosion of colours against a grey strip of gentrified Kitsilano, the usual mix of Whole Foods and Urban Outfitters. Lefebvre's face lights up and he shouts, "Hey!" and gives her the thumbs up. The woman laughs and smiles and waves at him as she sashays down the street. At first I think they know each other, but then I realize he's just showing her his appreciation. Another time, we are in the same café when an elderly man walks in wearing nothing but a long fluffy blue bathrobe and slippers. He sits down and orders lunch, obviously a regular because the formal waiters don't flinch. Lefebvre is delighted. We both admire the man's too-old-to-give-a-shit approach to life. With his cell phone, Lefebvre discreetly takes a photo for Hilary, his fourth wife.

He enjoys the characters, perhaps because he too is one. He's always worn his hair long, and when the company that made him rich—Neteller, an online money transfer service launched in the late nineties—was hitting its stride, he dressed like he was a dude waiting for the surf. As a fledgling musician, when he'd play on stage he'd wear sequin-covered suits made in Nashville, like those worn by country singers. He has a contagious laugh, and a bookish voice, the kind you might hear on public radio. As do a lot of hippies who've spent many hours tripping, he likes to talk about consciousness. He's articulate and often speaks with a formal parlance. He likes to prod friends who don't share his political views. He's playful, he bores easily and he refuses to toe the line. While his male friends tend to call him Johnny, his female friends call him John.

But he can get pensive too, and sullen, so that you don't know what he's thinking. There are things that he's unloading these days because he finds them burdensome. He calls the spectacular oceanfront real estate he owns "a headache," including Stonehouse, which he's listed on the international market. And he's downsizing in other ways. He's planning to sell the waterfront acreage where he and Hilary live, and to build a smaller house on the lot he owns next door. It will be tucked further back among the trees, but it will still have the oceanfront view, two small waterfalls and a tennis court. This is the plan. He regards this as simplifying and streamlining his life. Pricey acreage comes with too many responsibilities, he tells me. "I look forward to living the remaining years of my life free of that responsibility, among others."

Around the time Lefebvre got rich, *Forbes* magazine, which has made it a mission to track and define wealth as best it can, said, "Today, in terms of London or Parisian splendour, a magnate who has $300 million to his name can comfortably be considered among the superrich and can conduct himself accordingly." Lefebvre's idea of conducting himself accordingly was to part with almost all of it, as if he were the guinea pig in an experiment on rapid acquisition and equally rapid dissipation. I'd give an exact number if I could, but Lefebvre says he doesn't keep track of such things.

In the spring of 2019, he asked me to write a book about his life and his views, specifically his views on how the world should conduct itself. I met with him and his part-time business adviser, a man named Donald Mackenzie, whose work involves random projects for rich people. I'd met Mackenzie before, so I knew the trim, stylishly dressed figure to look for when I entered the art gallery café. He wore black-framed hexagon-shaped glasses and a paisley tie and greeted me with a hug. Mackenzie is a business consultant and lives in a big house with his husband outside the city; he also owns a pied-à-terre downtown. When he lived in London, England, years ago, he and his partner lived in singer Freddie Mercury's mansion for the last two years of the singer's life. Mackenzie once showed me a picture of Mercury wearing a bespoke vest covered in cat images that he had made for the singer one Christmas.

When Lefebvre walked in and sat down, I was taken aback by the long grey hair and man purse. He does not look like most people; he is a throwback to another era. He was gregarious and direct, and extremely keen that I sign onto the project. "It could make you famous," he said.

I knew nothing of Lefebvre's story until I did a little research and found the details of his involvement in Neteller, an electronic money transfer service that enabled online gamblers and bookies to make easy global transactions. A friend and client had come up with the idea, and Lefebvre, looking for another opportunity that wasn't law, joined in. They stumbled upon this idea at the tail end of the dot-com bubble, which was a six-year spree that lasted until 2000, during which time thousands of start-up tech companies seized on the rapid mainstream growth of this ballooning new thing called the Internet. Fuelled by intense speculation, entrepreneurs were becoming instant millionaires from unproven dot-com companies that expanded too soon by selling shares to the eager public. People quit their jobs and became full-time day traders, buying and selling tech stocks. Stories about the lavish lifestyles of instant millionaires drove the hype. But by 2002, the dot-com bubble burst, the venture capital dried up, and a lot of average people lost a lot of money on dot-com company investments.

At the time, I worked at a daily newspaper and, as part of the coverage of the 2004 Canadian federal election, I interviewed a hot dog truck operator who told me he'd lost $700,000 in the dot-com bust, wiping out his life savings. Hence, the hot dogs. The companies that tried to make big money fast were the ones that went under; the ones that played it safe and found a modestly scalable Internet niche business survived. I read in the *New York Times* that professors from the University of Maryland and the University of California, San Diego, sifted through email archives from the era and found that a surprising 48 per cent of Internet companies had scraped by. It hadn't been a total bust.

Neteller followed the standard dot-com formula of achieving growth as big and fast as possible. Lefebvre, along with a business partner named Steve Lawrence and a few initial investors, had hit his own jackpot by recognizing a lucrative niche, jumping on it and, within a few years, generating hundreds of millions in revenues. He was a hippie lawyer who'd stumbled into tech.

More interesting was his complex relationship to money. Ironically, Lefebvre had become a member of the rich people club that had offended him as a young lawyer. He could rub elbows with those people he sought to rattle. But he didn't just join the club that was making six or seven digits, he joined the rarefied air of the phenomenally rich— those people whose bank account numbers are so high that the numbers lose their meaning and context. If you have $30 million, it's still relatable—you can buy a mansion and a yacht and go for Michelin-star dinners every weekend. Most of us can get our heads around that. But if you have hundreds of millions, you buy airplanes and islands, the things that only characters in movies do. That's a whole other constellation of wealth. Lefebvre was in that category.

Money had a strange and yet predictable effect on Lefebvre. Once he became extremely rich, he developed an impressive disregard for the maxim to save more than you spend. He offloads money like he's tossing beads from a Mardi Gras float. I should qualify that: there was a time when he would throw money around so freely. These days, things have considerably slowed. But ask any of his friends or colleagues and they'll all agree that Lefebvre is terrible with money. Once I got to know him a little, and prodded as politely as I could about his fiscal recklessness, I discovered that he believes he is, in fact, "the best there is" with money.

The details of where his money has gone are hazy. It's not clear even to him where it went, but now he's down to the last few million. He continues to spend it, though he has a growing sense of the diminution of his wealth, which is mostly tied up in art and real estate—assets that are highly elastic. The private jet is long gone, as is the hangar, and the pilot he once employed, and the beach houses in Malibu. The story of Lefebvre isn't just a story about money but of how the money found its way into so many places that changed lives, helped foreign countries and changed the conversation around climate change—which is huge. And then there's the money that went to so many people and things that were totally useless too and didn't grow, so much so that it can't go to the good causes anymore. The downsizing and streamlining of his lifestyle, even selling off part of his beloved art collection, doesn't seem to faze him too much. If it does, he doesn't show it. That's not to say there aren't regrets. He has some of those, particularly giving money to the people who were undeserving, the ones who took advantage and played him, who were disdainful of his generosity. That part annoys him deeply. But you don't quite feel sorry for a man who's down to his last few million. And he doesn't expect sympathy.

It strikes me that Lefebvre might be living proof of the abundance mindset, territory well covered by Oprah. Hollywood self-help guru Deepak Chopra talks about the idea that if you believe the world is abundant, it will reward you. But believe in scarcity, and you'll spend your life scraping by. I've never been sure how this practice is implemented in the day to day, but there is something comforting in the thought that if you just tweak your own thinking, the rest will fall into place. There's an element of surrender involved that most of us can't fathom—after all, that credit card bill won't pay itself. Lefebvre just might be a bona fide case of surrendering it all to the gods of abundance. He has no fear that living like there's no tomorrow could mean a disastrous tomorrow. He's never had that fear in his life, even when he was broke and in debt to his friends and family for tens of thousands of dollars, and busking for his breakfast when he could have been practising law. When I ask him if he fears running out of money, he says he's got friends and family who won't let him fall, that there is always someone there to save him, and that his intuition has always served him well. In other words, he has no regrets looking back and he has no fears looking forward. "For me, 'me' has always been a bet that paid out well enough," he says.

He didn't do what was expected in several aspects: he didn't become a career lawyer; he didn't get married and settle down with one person for a lifetime (or at least, not until much later); he didn't save his money; he didn't work his way up a corporate ladder; he didn't fret about his future. One friend of his, a physicist named Victor Chan, writes books with the Dalai Lama and is founder of the Dalai Lama Center for Peace and Education, in Vancouver, of which Lefebvre is the founding patron. A friend of his, Jim Hoggan, connected Lefebvre to Chan, and Chan introduced him to the Tibetan spiritual leader. Chan has known the Dalai Lama since 1972, back when he travelled the world and ventured into Afghanistan, where he and a group of other young people were kidnapped and held hostage for several days. He befriended one of his female co-captives, and when they escaped she took him to Tibet to meet the Dalai Lama. If it weren't for the ordeal, he'd never have met His Holiness, he says, and he'd never have gone on to work with him all these decades later. Chan says that he shares the same disregard for material possessions as Lefebvre, because they are both hippies who truly believed the hippie mantra of peace and love. They smoked hash, they listened to rock 'n' roll, and they were strongly influenced by the messages of civil unrest and the Vietnam protest years. "Of course, we want to survive, but you tend to have less attachment to money and less attachment to things, to toys," Chan says.

Everyone, including the man himself, agrees that Lefebvre got lucky. Environmental activist, scientist and media personality David Suzuki has known Lefebvre for more than a decade and says he's always thought that Lefebvre had an unusual attitude toward his wealth. "He knew he had lucked into this thing. My feeling was that he was overwhelmed, because suddenly he was a very wealthy man. He could do things he never dreamed of—but he didn't think he deserved to be this super wealthy guy. That's the way it is with the digital revolution, you get these people who have an idea, and maybe one out of a thousand or even less scores big time. And when they do, it's a big deal."

Lefebvre made the money at a time when the dot-com world was falling apart, when investors were taking huge losses and start-ups were failing. But Neteller had tapped into an astonishing glut of revenue, one that wouldn't stop bubbling upward, at a time when other companies were slowing down if not entirely tanking. The story of Neteller isn't just the story of Lefebvre. It's the story of a group of men (and they were men) who helped build a business out of nothing in only a few years, and of how they then sold off shares, made other investments, and saved and grew their money so that they'd never have to worry about it again. Today, they are all multi-millionaires and, as far as money goes anyway, seemingly fulfilled—and then there's their friend Lefebvre, who didn't look so far ahead and who offloaded his money for what he saw as a higher purpose.

He had the kind of money that should never have come to him, but it did, weirdly. And so, here we are today, looking at the remaining fruits of that $350 million that came to him perhaps a little too easily—and too freely. After all, does anyone actually deserve that kind of money? That's another question. When I described the book project, and Lefebvre's outrageous offloading of his wealth, to an academic friend who has a visionary take on the world as well as an impressive track record for his own tech investments, he said, "Is he self-destructive or is he self-constructive? Is he foolish for giving his money away, or are we foolish for thinking it will redeem us? Perhaps he's a modern-day Buddha, dispensing with all his worldly goods because he knows there is far more to it."

TWO

Making Money

IN 2006, AT a black-tie affair in a hotel ballroom in downtown Vancouver, John Lefebvre is bidding on an Arkansas recipe book donated by U.S. president Bill Clinton, who is in attendance. It is the annual fundraiser by Diana Krall & Friends for Vancouver General Hospital, in memory of her mother, Adella, who had died from lymphoma a few years before. Krall is there, alongside husband Elvis Costello, and Elton John. Lefebvre started the bidding and then kept bidding until it got to around $3,000, at which point everyone dropped out except for him. A ripple of surprise moves over the room of five hundred or so affluent guests as they watch the man in the tux with long grey hair continue to bid against himself, going up to $5,000. Lefebvre is delighted he's created a stir. He yells out: "Come on, people, what did we come here for?" He ultimately bids up the price and "wins" the little Clinton book for $17,000. It wasn't an isolated incident. Many times, Lefebvre would bid against himself, or outbid rooms full of people for charity auction items, whether they were valuable art pieces or items of little or no value, sometimes giving the item as a gift to the other bidder. Or he'd buy all the raffle tickets for an event that was underselling. One time, Lefebvre recalls that while he was bidding against himself at a dressy fundraiser, he was seated across the table from Chip Wilson, the billionaire founder of clothing line Lululemon Athletica. Wilson turned in his seat: "Who the hell is this guy?"

JOHN LEFEBVRE'S WORLDVIEW was shaped largely by his upbringing. Lefebvre's father, a soldier, had died when Lefebvre was three years old. They had moved around Canada because of his father's army job, but at the time they were living in Chatham, New Brunswick. Driving home one night, the senior Lefebvre encountered a blizzard, so he and several other drivers pulled over to the side of the road. An army man, he knew what to do to survive. He turned off the engine and wrapped himself in a blanket to wait out the storm. But the car in front of him had backed up close to his bumper, and the driver kept the engine running to warm his family. By morning, Lefebvre's father had died from asphyxiation from carbon monoxide poisoning. "I remember being home, and my mom was concerned about something because Dad wasn't home. It was dark out; there was a knock at the door and two soldiers stood there, a colonel and a padre. They told my sister, brother and me to go play in another room."

His grief-stricken mother immediately moved Lefebvre and his two siblings to Calgary, where she had grown up. They purchased a beautiful house in a leafy neighbourhood near the river, and the family settled there until Lefebvre's teen years. Her late husband had been senior enough that she pulled in a good pension from his army service, including free university tuition for herself. She went to the University of Alberta in Calgary, or UAC, as it was called in 1962, and she got a teaching degree and became a high school teacher. Later, she went back to school and became a counsellor at St. Mary's Girl's High School. Lefebvre recalls an idyllic childhood, though he and his siblings would "run wild," which caused their mother some stress. When the river froze over, the neighbourhood kids would skate on it, or create hockey rinks out of small ponds. In his teen years, when his mother went away for a few weeks to attend university out of town, he would throw wild parties.

His mother's devout Catholicism was of the kind that encouraged theological debate about the conscious choice we make to do good or evil, and why Catholics are not superior to anyone else. They were raised on the "leading edge" of a more progressive Catholicism in the early 1960s. That progressive new take on religion, combined with the rock 'n' roll revolution, greatly informed Lefebvre. A regular at the house was Father Pat O'Byrne, an intellectual leader in ecumenism, or unity among different faith groups, who ran a social services program out of the church. In the early 1960s, when Lefebvre was a young teenager, O'Byrne introduced the Lefebvre family to famous French philosopher and Jesuit priest Pierre Teilhard de Chardin, whose then-radical teachings on the coexistence of Christianity and science have been cited by popes since he died. The young Lefebvre also started reading the works of Father Andrew Greeley, an American sociologist, journalist and prolific author, and an outspoken critic of American Catholicism, who had an unfiltered view of sexuality. "Their teachings helped convince me that whatever else the Church was doing wrong, there were wonderful spiritual thinkers involved, and you couldn't tar them all with the same brush," says Lefebvre. "And I came to embrace what I realized to be very important lessons of morality from my exposure to Catholicism when I was younger. My fundamental moral view is the one that I believe most properly represents what Jesus was teaching, and that was 'Everybody gets the same chance at the love of the universe, and come early or come late, the prize is still the same. What you do for the least [of people] you do for me.' But don't think you've fulfilled your requirement by giving alms, because giving alms is just avoiding doing the hard parts of love, which is joining in the community, listening to people, caring about them, making friends and helping them emotionally as well. He called it 'healing.' It's not the most widely accepted view of what Jesus taught, but if you look carefully, it was the truest essence of what the guy was laying down for us."

To understand a bit more about John Lefebvre, a few recurring themes need exploration, including drugs, music and his philosophy on life. They've been the consistent backdrop, even after his fortuitous stumbling into the Internet business—which altered his life so radically that, to the observer, it would have looked like an event from someone else's life. Let's start with drugs, which intertwine with his passion for both music and philosophy. Lefebvre's early memories of taking drugs are enmeshed with the songs played on the radio when he was a young man, still a boy, really: Cream's "Sunshine of Your Love," the Doors' "Light My Fire," Buffalo Springfield's "For What It's Worth," The Rascals' "It's a Beautiful Morning." He and his friends would climb a big tree on a quiet hillside street that they nicknamed Arthur, sit on Arthur's thick branches, smoke a joint and trip on acid or mescaline, and stare into the sky for hours. High and starving, they would go for pizza at Ye Olde Pizza Joint, sit at gingham-cloth-covered tables and play their favourite songs on the jukebox. In those moments, tripping with his friends and the music, and with the subculture they'd helped define, Lefebvre felt like he was part of a unified purpose. He felt liberated. He felt like he was going to be a young, morally unconventional badass revolutionary forever.

"Everybody knew what everybody else in the whole world was doing at that very moment," he recalls. "We knew exactly what we were doing to exactly the same soundtrack. We unified the entire planet with one vision, one consciousness. There would be no stopping us. We would make the world strawberry fields. At the end of the Beatles' White Album, when Ringo says 'Goodnight everybody, everybody everywhere,' we were exactly who was listening."

At age seventeen, he was living with about a dozen hippies in a big five-bedroom house near the Bow River. Because they were regularly dropping acid, they began dealing it. It only made sense. They needed the money, and they had ready access to customers—their friends and acquaintances. Two of his roommates were serious dealers, but Lefebvre was a dealer only in the sense that he'd answer the door to anyone looking for it, and help facilitate the transaction. "That one summer in 1969, I think they sold twenty thousand hits of acid," he says. "If somebody came to the door and said, 'Have you got acid?' I would say, 'Sure, probably' and then go off and get it. I never made money selling it, but I lived off the people who were selling acid, so I felt it was the least I could do to lend a hand on the distribution end." In a kitchen cupboard, they kept a bucket stashed with communal money. The guys who were making the most income in the house—the official drug dealers—were the biggest contributors to the bucket, and nobody ever took advantage and made off with all the money, says Lefebvre. They were living true to their values of sharing the wealth.

"Ever hear of the Diggers?" he asks me by way of comparison. I hadn't, so I looked them up. It turns out that the Diggers were an anonymous group of young, theatrical anarchists living in San Francisco's famous hippie mecca, the Haight-Ashbury neighbourhood. They were down on authority, money and capitalism, and up with free health care, transit, food, concerts, art and housing. Basically, everything should be free, and the lines between the haves and have-nots eradicated. They walked the walk too, giving out food that was either donated or stolen to hundreds of people each day at Golden Gate Park, or from soup kitchens that they ran. Impressively, they coined the phrase "Today is the first day of the rest of your life." Not so impressively, although the Diggers may have preached equal rights, they seemed less concerned about equality of the sexes. The counterculture movement of the '60s, and the commune life that was part of it, wasn't as revolutionary for the women as it had been for the men. Women were the ones who cooked the food and served it up, went along with no-strings sex and cared for the kids, while the guys got to come up with the ideas, make the big decisions and bask in their new-found freedom.

One day, when the roommates were just about to jump in their cars and drive to Woodstock, New York, for the famous outdoor festival, the police made a surprise appearance at the hippie house on the Bow. The young men had been the subject of an undercover operation in which three police officers had posed as acid users. "I was scared shit-less," says Lefebvre. At the city jail, they waited on a bench to be booked. Lefebvre watched as the police booked and searched his friends, one by one. He realized that in his haste to get dressed he'd put on his roommate's jeans. He shoved his hands into the pockets to make sure there was nothing incriminating to be found, and he felt pills. He discreetly pulled out two hits of lime green acid. A hot panic washed over him.

He dug his elbow into the friend next to him.

"What? Oh," said the friend, looking down at the little pills Lefebvre held in his hand.

They looked at each other.

Lefebvre took one hit and his friend took the other.

After he got bailed out two days later, Lefebvre was charged with drug dealing. He spent eight months inside the Bowden Institution in the town of Innisfail, north of Calgary. Bowden was new at the time and not yet the more serious federal institution it would become in the mid-1970s. Compared with his friends, who were serving two years' time or more, Lefebvre got off easy. It wasn't as pleasant as a summer camp, but he had plenty of buddies to play cards with while they sat around in jail, bored out of their minds, and slightly terrified of the hardened inmates.

Lefebvre's mother, Louise, who was heartbroken by her son's situation, had pulled some social strings with a friend in the judicial system to help her son get a lighter sentence. Lefebvre says his mother believed in his innate goodness. "She was very concerned that I was giving my life over to drugs and stuff. I knew she was wrong, but I couldn't convince her otherwise. She was super courageous, because she understood that whatever else was happening, I was no idiot. She did strongly believe I had been misled." Louise wasn't a pushover, though. To prevent her son from freeloading off her after his release, she moved from the house into a small apartment, he tells me, laughing.

The prison warden might have been less convinced of Lefebvre's innocence. Although Lefebvre had served his minimum time, the warden didn't free him until a once-in-your-lifetime rock festival featuring Janis Joplin and the Grateful Dead had passed through town, that summer of 1970 (footage of that tour was later made into the music documentary *Festival Express*). Lefebvre was angry. He felt ripped off. To this day, he is convinced it was a deliberate move to make sure he missed out on the fun. But his mother's connections weren't enough. After being freed, the Crown appealed to prolong his sentence. His lawyer, Milt Harradence, insisted he enrol right away in university, in order to present himself to the judge as a sincere young man trying to make something of himself. The ruse worked. The Crown appeal was dismissed, and Lefebvre stumbled into post-secondary education. It wasn't a direct route to academia, however, because Lefebvre didn't really want to study. He blew that first year, skipping class to play bridge with friends, hanging at smoky bars, smoking his fair share of pot and hash too, and generally living the life of a turned-on, tuned-in dropout. But the counterculture revolution that informed youth to "drop acid, not bombs" began to enter a dark phase. He saw friends delve into harder drugs, such as heroin. "It got really scuzzy really quickly," he says. He'd spent years wasted and high, working at odd jobs like gardening, building forms on construction sites and driving a late-night taxi, drunks and rough types as his customers. One time a guy in the backseat pulled a gun on the guy sitting next to Lefebvre, in the passenger seat. Lefebvre, who was "scared shitless," did as he was told, dropping his front-seat passenger off at the next corner (he was pleased to get out) and the others later in an alley. They wished him well and tipped him handsomely. Events like that took their toll, and he soon came to see that he needed a more ordered life.

He finally went back to university—slowly at first, taking night school courses. And then, at age twenty-seven, a mature student, he enrolled full time. A keen reader, and always up for a debate, he became intrigued with the study of law.

At the University of Calgary, Lefebvre set his future in motion as a popular student who knew how to sway people. After his second year, in 1978, he was elected president of the student union. It was the most ambitious move he'd ever made. Presiding over the student union is the standard path to climbing the corporate ladder because you establish contacts with other A-type students, you meet leaders you'd otherwise never meet, and your campus leadership gives you the skills required to manage employees. You also get paid.

But Lefebvre didn't care about the executive corporate ladder or lifestyle. He was more motivated by the chance to be seen in the starring role as the student union president. He got attention. He figured it would also help with his admittance to law school. Lefebvre had never even been on a student council before, and he served as president for only one year. But during his stint, he met Prime Minister Pierre Elliott Trudeau, and joined him and other university executives for a stroll across the campus, with huge crowds of onlookers. Trudeau was a respected intellectual who didn't suffer fools. Lefebvre was impressed with his easy confidence, even though many Albertans despised him for the National Energy Program, which had placed a cap on the price of oil that Albertans could sell to the rest of Canada. They saw it as an unfair hit to Alberta, costing them billions for the benefit of eastern industry. Trudeau was impervious to the students who booed him. "He was entitled, but he knew how to act like he wasn't," says Lefebvre. "Somebody asked him if he ever smoked pot, and he said, 'You mean in Canada?' He had a wicked wit. He reminded me of the people my mom hung out with, which is to say, proudly intellectual. And by that, I mean well read."

While school president, Lefebvre had met a young nurse named Katharine. Katharine was eight months pregnant with their daughter, Emily, when they married on Halloween night 1980, at her parents' house. Lefebvre graduated law school in 1982 and was called to the bar a year later. He had enjoyed studying law, but the reality of working as a lawyer was less enticing. But he had to do something because all his friends were getting on with their careers, and besides, he now had a family. "I had to get a job, and I didn't have much science or math," he says. "I just knew all my friends were on track to better themselves, and I felt conspicuous."

He took an articling position with law firm McCaffery and Company, which specialized in foreclosures—big business during the 1980s recession. After he was called to the bar, he felt obliged to stay at McCaffrey awhile, since they had trained him. Lefebvre tried to fit into the corporate world: for a short time, he cut his hair shorter and he put on a three-piece navy blue suit every day. But he felt hemmed in. The work for the firm's juniors was either mind-numbing, detail-oriented research or on things like pork industry price-fixing prosecution, an assignment that took him through his first couple of years. It was interesting enough, but he knew the work would never amount to a transferable skill set. "Day to day, it did not do anything for the part of me that just spent eight years dropping acid, playing music, listening to brilliant stoned philosophers and doing whatever the fuck I wanted in the universe."

Lefebvre believes that great ideas are often born through drug use, and his philosophic bent has carried him through the decades. His upbringing with a devout Catholic for a mother, and listening in on dinner-party discussions about the meaning of Christ's teachings, meant his acid use took him on a particularly spiritual journey. And perhaps because she encouraged a philosophical, broadly catholic view of life, and questioning the nature of society and existence, he developed a disdain for convention. "To me, the essential experience of getting your mind blown is understanding that the consciousness we experience, more profoundly when we are high on acid, is actually the same thing in all of us. The human experience is that we have become smarter through evolution to the point where we have become conscious of our being, and when we attained that consciousness, we became part of a single thing that is ubiquitous throughout the universe, that we, somewhat dismissively, call consciousness."

At the day-to-day superficial level, Lefebvre was as uncommitted to his young personal life as he was to his work. While at McCaffrey, Lefebvre's marriage fell apart. "I think I am pretty grown-up now, but being a responsible partner was hard for me. Life is a very long curriculum," he says.

Calgary, Alberta, would have had a population of only about 620,000 in 1985, and other than doubling in people and office towers in the intervening years, the city is still the Canadian Dallas because of its oil, its wealth, its cowboys and its decades of voting for conservative governments. Law circles in any city have little room for rebellious, attention-seeking behaviour. But Lefebvre, attending a reception for a colleague's call to the bar, sought attention. There was extroverted Lefebvre, six foot one and thirty-four years old, wearing a tweedy casual blazer that he got from Woodward's department store, a glass of Scotch in hand, eyes glazed from the doobie smoked an hour prior, laughing easily as he moved from person to person. He loved a party. When it came to women especially, he displayed a surfeit of confidence, and he disarmed them with a hearty, good-natured focus that made them feel special.

At the party, he eventually made his way to a young lawyer named Jane Bergman.

She'd seen him before, at the University of Calgary, where she was two years behind him in law school. You couldn't miss him, she says. "He was at the party wearing eyeliner."

They struck up an immediately flirty conversation that was the beginning of an on-again-off-again romance and work partnership that would go on for years. "I know you," he said to Jane, who was eating a cookie. He made a joke about the cookie making her fat. She was not coy: "I should just slap this onto my boobs. That's where I could use it."

Lefebvre had at the time separated with the mother of his baby daughter. He and Jane were soon living together, and eventually they decided to quit working for other law firms to start their own grassroots-style firm for the people. They leased space in a former art gallery outside the city's downtown core, an old brick warehouse-type operation with high ceilings. They got a bank loan and help from Jane's parents, who used equity in their house to finance the couple's new business. The deal caused Jane a lot of anxiety. She was from a modest background. Her father had been a house painter and her mother a stay-at-home mom.

Lefebvre designed the office interior as a faux streetscape, like the set for a TV show, with a park and park bench, old-fashioned globe streetlights and plants at the reception area, and he transformed each of the lawyer offices into little houses with roofs. The colour palette would have been a jarring juxtaposition to the standard-issue beige decor of most corporate law firms. Theirs was the world of law through a kaleidoscope hippie lens: the boardroom was a burgundy coloured house with a blue roof. The law clinic was also the first of many elaborate Lefebvre interior designs, and he'd done a lot with a small budget. Later, when he could afford expensive things, he'd live in a barnboard house with large paintings by well-known artists covering the walls and multicoloured pashminas fastened between the beams on the cathedral-high ceiling. For now, he had an old-timey Main Street office space. "The interior design was the best part of that practice," he says, "apart from the fact I could be at ease drinking wine by early Friday afternoon and take most weekends off."

They gave their law firm a quirky homespun name, the Sunnyside Legal Clinic. The Law Society of Alberta initially challenged their informal branding but eventually relaxed a requirement that said lawyers must name their companies using their surnames, which opened the door to other firms doing the same. And so Lefebvre and Jane led the way for unconventional lawyers who wanted to take the formality out of their profession. They didn't have to exist under the starchy Lefebvre Bergman, Barristers and Solicitors. In keeping with their grassroots mission, they took almost any case that came through their colourful offices, with Lefebvre doing criminal defence, small business and real estate conveyancing and mortgage financing. Their work hours generally stuck to the typical forty-hour weeks, unlike the seventy-hour weeks their contemporaries were pulling downtown. "We were just trying to make enough money in a reasonable amount of time so that we could actually have a life. Jane made better than a teacher [salary], and I did less than a teacher. But I supplemented that with the odd small toke transaction."

The elderly lady who owned their office building died, and because she had liked her young tenants, her family offered them the opportunity to purchase the property. Lefebvre and Jane knew that, at $100,000, they would be getting it far below value, so they scraped together the money to purchase it and then flipped it eight months later. They made a $40,000 profit, which was a year's income for each of them at the time. In those days, they were getting financing wherever they could find it. As well, they had mounting debts that included student loans. Once they sold off the building, they then leased the space back from the new owner.

By 1990, their firm grew to six lawyers. But the schedule was gruelling, even for a worker bee like Jane. As for Lefebvre, working in a law clinic with an upbeat name and a look like something on *Sesame Street* didn't inspire him any more than McCaffery had. Jane was thirty years old and Lefebvre was thirty-eight. She wanted to travel and enjoy her youth, so they leased out their house, sold off their business and Lefebvre cashed out his registered retirement savings. They used the money to travel to India and Thailand for five months. The trip would edge Lefebvre away from a law career and toward something entirely out of left field. In Mumbai (then known as Bombay), they met up with a friend of a former client named Raju, who was importing cheap leather goods to Canada. Intrigued, Lefebvre returned to India a few months later to investigate his own leather-importing opportunity. He brought along some nice leather jackets that he wanted Raju to replicate, and he took a tour of the factory. Lefebvre was willing to take the risk of a new business, despite not having any import or retail experience. "I decided I would rather go broke selling leather jackets than practise law," says Lefebvre.

In 1993, Lefebvre started a leather goods shop. Jane had her doubts about the venture, and so did their friend Bruce Ramsay. "John is not the most fiscally acute person," says Jane. But as was his custom, Lefebvre ignored their protestations and pushed through on the idea. "The plan was to completely have faith in Raju and the quality of his product. If I built it, they would come—in both those things I was quite wrong." He opened a shop on a gentrified street and called the store Saviour Skin, painting the interior a vibrant red and green. "It seemed earthy and stoned all at the same time," he says. He had hoped to get his first shipment in September, in time for the Christmas shopping season, but it didn't arrive until a couple of weeks before Christmas. And when he opened the boxes, the designs were a disappointment. They were cheap looking knock-offs, and some of the jackets were made of leather as stiff as beef jerky. He managed to sell a few of the old air force–style jackets with fur-trimmed collars to the boys from the snowboard shop next door, but only about a dozen or so. Otherwise, nothing was selling. Lefebvre worked at the shop alone twelve hours a day, seven days a week, waiting for customers who never came. But he wasn't panicked about his failure to turn a profit: he spent his long days smoking dope and writing a novel about a spy who became an international diamond smuggler. He wanted to be a writer, but he also knew he didn't have the chops to complete his novel. "I devoted most of my time to the book rather than making the store work." After about a year, Jane left him and the business closed. He could no longer make the payments for the jackets coming from India, so Raju applied for a court order and arrived with a sheriff one day to seize merchandise. He cleared out about 90 per cent of the store, which shut down the business. Lefebvre lost about $70,000, including the $25,000 he had borrowed from his law-school friend Murray Pettem and the $17,000 or so he'd got from the sale of his house. "I didn't feel too upset," he says. "I knew whose fault it was. It was me trying to avoid responsibility." Jane describes him as one of the most insecure people she knows. She would tell friends that she felt like she was living with Peter Pan. His enthusiasm was infectious, and endearing, she says, but she also found him groundless, living in a fantasyland.

Still, Jane saw that he was low on cash and invited him to practise at the new law firm she had been running from sub-leased space inside an insurance office. Her partner at the firm had left, so she asked Lefebvre if he'd like to join her. He came on board, and they also tried to rekindle their romance. It all blew up pretty quickly.

Lefebvre tried to fit into the corporate world, but his personality often got in the way. Two guys he'd met from university had started a company chartering houseboats. People would invest in hundreds of the large boats, using them for themselves like a time-share, and then the rest of the time, having the boats chartered out. The company was doing the same thing with condominiums, finding investors and then renting out their units. Investors didn't have to deal with the hassles of hiring property managers. The men were going public with the venture and needed more in-house counsel, and they invited Lefebvre to join them to do purchaser relations. So, late one night, Lefebvre packed up his things at the office he shared with Jane and left without telling her. He lasted six months at the new company before he told the VP of finance to "go fuck himself." Not surprisingly, the VP fired him on the spot. On his way out, he passed by a colleague's office and the man shouted, "John, tell me you knew that nobody tells Al to 'Go fuck himself'?" Lefebvre laughs when he tells me this story. He wants me to understand that his principles took precedence over any stupid job. He wasn't going to play the game. As his friends would later learn when they tried to help him win the game of growing money—as opposed to depleting it—along with principles, he's also got a streak of obstinacy.

Before he'd pulled the midnight run on Jane, he had attended a company baseball game with the employees from the insurance office. While on the diamond, he met a woman named Karen Fowlie. She was in her twenties and working in insurance but really wanted to make it as a singer. This intrigued Lefebvre, as his main passion was music. He was forty-six years old, without any money to show for his years of scraping by as a lawyer, in a profession he detested for himself. In what his friends saw as a midlife crisis, he threw himself into playing music with Fowlie. "I didn't give a shit what anybody thought of me anymore. I was too far gone to care. I knew everything that was in that world, everything that came from it, and I wanted none of it, all the phony golf memberships and private club memberships, and trying to fit in with an elite community. I felt like a bull-shitter every time I went into those goddamn places. I felt like a complete charlatan. I was done before I was started."

The boat company job, though short-lived, had left him with some severance money, which allowed him to play music. Lefebvre had also developed a passion for songwriting. It was 1997, and he was a man who was going to live for the day: he was going to be a songwriting musician. He gave himself a challenge to write a song a day for seven days, and he taught Fowlie how to play guitar. They called themselves French Kiss the Fortune Teller, and played cover songs by Emmylou Harris, Lucinda Williams and Gram Parsons. On his guitar he played her "White Rabbit," which she'd never heard before, and he taught her to sing it. She nailed it. "Remember what the dormouse said—'feed your head.'"

They would play anywhere they could, coffee shops and open stages, for $50 a show, and they busked on the streets and in commuter train stations. Lefebvre would lay open his guitar case and nod at anybody who'd throw some change in. For a while, he found the hand-to-mouth busker life greatly appealing, and freeing. The duo would play bars into the wee hours of the night, drinking and smoking pot, then head out for Chinese food before returning to their respective homes to catch a few hours' sleep. In the morning, they would hit the train station to play for commuters. Occasionally, in the train station by the university, he'd see a professor or administrator he recognized, but they never looked at him. The professionals and businesspeople never acknowledged their existence, he says, but the working-class service workers did. "They understood from being out in the world that playing music is an honourable profession, whereas the people from the posh end of town would treat you like a fucking beggar. As if that were a bad thing." After the morning rush, the duo would get bacon and eggs, sleep all day, write songs and then head back out for the end-of-day rush-hour crowd. "I liked living like a bohemian," he says. "It's so beautiful not to have anything that you have to do except go out and sing and hang out and get high and, you know, just keep it all cool."

He wasn't worried about money because he'd borrowed $30,000 from his mother, to purchase a condo. He also had the lease on the new Toyota RAV4 Crossover SUV. "I was just being irresponsible, really," he tells me. But he and Fowlie were serious too about their efforts. With the help of Calgary bass player and producer Danny Patton, they made an album. They would stack copies of their CD by Lefebvre's guitar case when they busked, but people rarely bought it. So he gave them away to friends and family. After nearly two years of performing around town, Lefebvre started to lose interest in playing coffee shops, dives and train platforms. To supplement his income, he had picked up work for a small company called Go Cards, which sold ad space on postcards that were then distributed to businesses. The cards were a familiar sight in the reception areas of restaurants, hair salons and shops. When Lefebvre had his business card printed, he chose the job title "human being." "The owner thought it was cool," he says, laughing. But his friends were starting to wonder where he was headed. He worked for Go Cards for six months before admitting that it was foolish not to make use of his legal training. He owed about $60,000 to friends and family. He reasoned to himself, "[I] could just be a lawyer until I could pay back some of my debts and pay my own way." He started doing the odd legal job off the side of his desk, mostly for his buddy Steve Lawrence, a real estate developer. He had first met Lawrence while sharing office space with Jane. Lawrence was one of her clients, and she'd asked Lefebvre to handle the conveyancing work for Lawrence's real estate deals. Lawrence was a small-time commercial real estate developer who built multi-family dwellings and strip malls, including one with a car wash. Lawrence sold all the retail spaces in the strip mall except for the car wash, because he recognized it was a nice little cash cow, says Lefebvre. The two hit it off and became friends. Together they would drink good whisky and talk about various ways of making money. They were also united by a love of music, partying, cigars and poker. Lawrence was a hard-core Frank Zappa fan. "He really liked people who were out of bounds. In some ways, Steve was a man of very acute tastes."

Jane, the ever-patient friend (to a fault), could see that Lefebvre was struggling, so she also offered him legal work. She needed help too. By this time, she had married and become Jane McMullen, and she was pregnant and would be on maternity leave soon. She asked Lefebvre to take over her small practice so she could keep it going for when she returned. "John's music career wasn't generating revenue, so he was pretty penniless at that point. I said, 'Listen, I'm going to quit and go on mat leave. Do you want to take my practice while I'm away?'" Enticed by earning real money rather than busking for change or selling Go Cards space, he took her up on the offer.

Meanwhile, Lawrence had stumbled upon an idea he believed had potential, and he was excited.

At the car wash, Lawrence had hired a teenage employee named Jeff Natland to empty out the loonies in the machines and fill the soap dispensers. Natland was a clever computer programmer and budding Internet genius. (He declined an interview request for this book, and Lawrence is not reachable, so I have only Lefebvre's version of events to go by.) Natland told Lawrence he had been gambling online, using his dad's credit card, and Lawrence was intrigued. He asked the teenager if he could program a roulette or blackjack game. Natland said he probably could, and then did.

The developer and his whiz kid protege flew to San José, the capital and largest city of Costa Rica, on a six-month sojourn to start an online gambling business and learn the ropes. San José is a hotbed of hotel casino gambling and sex workers, and at the time, it was home to a large, sketchy community of online gambling businesses. The duo formed GambleUSA.com, a gambling site where gamblers could play standard casino games. However, they could see a ton of money flowing through the bookie betting system, especially sports betting, a highly lucrative but fiercely competitive business. And so they dove in. Bookies don't care if customers win or lose because they make their money on commission. When a person places a bet for $20, the bookie will take a cut, or a "vig" of, say, $2. If the person loses their bet, the $20 goes to the winner, and the bookie pockets $2 from both the winning and losing bets. But it's important that the bookies keep their bets balanced. If 80 per cent of their customers are betting on one team and the other team wins, the bookie would get killed paying off the winners. So bookies find other bookies who will "lay off bets." These other bookies have more bets on the opposite side, and they agree to cover each other's bets. Because they lay off bets, their books are balanced and they don't have to worry about waking up to a nightmare loss. They simply collect their commissions. Problem was, the two were novices, with hardly a clue about bookie culture.

They were way out of their depth. Lawrence and Natland didn't understand how betting "lines" worked, or what happened when the odds on games—called the point spread—changed, sometimes rapidly. And they didn't know how to respond.

There are different types of lines. The odds makers might declare a six-point spread bet, and the bookies would adopt the spread, which means your team has to win by six points in order for you to win the bet. A money line bet is when you just bet which team will win, and if the odds makers declare the odds are, say, three to one, you'd have to have bet $3 on the favourite to get back $4. The odds makers study the teams and create various lines and spreads in the weeks leading up to a game. What's important in that lead-up is that bookies watch each other closely and change the odds according to the latest information, so they're all pretty much in sync. For example, a key player might get injured, requiring a change to the line or the spread—or the weather forecast is poor, or a person in the know bets a lot of money on one team. Whatever the reason, the lines and the spreads can change right up until game time. Lawrence and Natland missed this important detail and so weren't changing their odds minute to minute with the odds makers. The experienced gamblers saw that Gamble USA was slow to adjust the odds, and so opportunists started betting from both sides. "They bet for one side on the lower odds and against them on the higher odds. It doesn't matter which way the game goes, they win the difference," says Lefebvre. "It's an arbitrage against the bookie, and the bookie gets killed."

Defeated, Lawrence gave up, sold the business for nothing, and headed back to Calgary. But before he left, he had met Nick Barlow, a U.S. online gambling entrepreneur who needed money transferred for his players. Lawrence let

Barlow use Gamble USA's Western Union Quick Collect account for a fee, and quickly realized that the industry was missing the crucial payments piece. Indeed, Lawrence had seen the problem firsthand while operating his own online gambling business. Bookies who used credit cards soon discovered that the world is teeming with hackers who break into websites and steal account information. But conventional cheques took too long to reach the bookies. Gamblers like to gamble in real time; they don't want two- or three-day delays in placing their bets. Having to place their bets several days in advance put them at a disadvantage if the bookie's lines shifted by game day. And if they won, it could take weeks to receive their winnings because the cheque the bookie sent would be drawn on a bank in Costa Rica.

Credit cards were the quickest option for paying a bookie, but they can't be used to send the cardholder their winnings. Moreover, credit cards were a source of fraud for the industry. People would call up the credit card company to report that those gambling charges weren't theirs, and demand that the charges be reversed. Those charge backs were costing the bookies a fortune. Bookies had a bad-debt rate as high as 15 or 20 per cent, which made it tough for them to do business. All in all, the people running the sites didn't have a way to make secure, reliable money transfers to and from their players, and it was costing them. Lawrence's gambling venture might have been a fiasco, but it was also the genesis for what would become a massive life-changing jackpot for all involved: an electronic-wallet platform called Neteller.

Lawrence realized that there was a niche he could fill facilitating the transactions between gambling companies and bookies and their customers. And if he took most of the risk away from the bookies, it would put them in good stead with the whole industry. Lefebvre says: "It came to Steve that if someone brought some responsibility and professionalism, some reliability and efficiency, to this money transfer side of online gaming, that would be a pretty good little business model. And Jeff goes, 'Yeah, and we could do it all on the Internet.' Instead of sending their credit card info to every bookie site, gamblers sent it to us, and we put their money in a Neteller account. Gamblers could bet from their own Neteller account, receive their winnings in it, and the bookie only has to settle with us once a week rather than complete separate money transfer transactions for every bet. We were the virtual bag man. And we took *all* of the bad-debt risk out of it. A Neteller dollar was a good dollar every time. The industry ate it up and forced their clients to use us, mostly because we managed the risk professionally. We ran bad-debt levels of about 0.3 per cent."

Lawrence explained the concept to Lefebvre, especially the huge potential of it. Lefebvre immediately wanted in on Lawrence's start-up. He dumped French Kiss and Jane's law practice. Jane, at home with a newborn, was furious that Lefebvre had bailed on her yet again. But the proposition of working with Lawrence and potentially becoming solvent was too good for Lefebvre to pass up. "John being John, he was off to do this Neteller thing and sort of abandoned my practice. Does he feel guilty? He should," she says with a laugh. The rawness of the episode has healed over with the years, and besides, Lefebvre did make it up to her. Eventually, he would make amends to everybody he'd let down in those years. For now, he gave her $25,000 for her trouble (that would be only a fraction of the compensation she'd receive from Lefebvre once he struck it rich).

"I walked away and she was very disappointed, because it was difficult for her to recover her practice after that," says Lefebvre. "But I was pretty much always dissatisfied with the practice of law. My compatriots had interesting legal careers, but mine wasn't one of them. I enjoyed visiting with clients and wasting time visiting with lawyers and all that stuff. But I wasn't good at putting my nose to the grindstone and my ass in the air. Jane was super disciplined. I preferred getting stoned.

"It wasn't massaging the part of my soul that needed the most attention."

That year, 1999, Lawrence had leased a former railway storage space with brick walls, wood floors and post-and-beam ceilings, on the floor above a steakhouse and a pub. Lefebvre came up with the name Neteller, a mashup of the words "Internet" and "teller." Lefebvre used his sales instincts to get investors on board, and visited a fringe bank in the Bahamas for support. He travelled to the U.S. to meet with bookies to learn the business. And he got start-up cash from his former roommate Bruce Ramsay, who wanted to see his friend get out from under his mountain of debt. A silent partner who prefers to remain anonymous to this day also came on board. Lefebvre is willing to say only that he was a successful restaurant and nightclub owner in Calgary. By the end of the year, they had the website up and running. Lawrence owned 65 per cent of the company; Lefebvre owned 35 per cent. They brought in investors, including a silent investor who invested $200,000 for capital costs. A year or so later, they gave Natland a couple of percentage points for his conceptual contribution. Early on, they knew that Natland would be leaving to start his own company in Silicon Valley, which was buzzing. The outside investors and sweat equity workers shared 29 per cent ownership in the business, with Lawrence and Lefebvre owning the remaining 71 per cent. The two founders continued to divide their stake 65/35, with Lawrence the biggest shareholder.

Lefebvre was soon working from 6 a.m. to midnight, seven days a week, as he threw himself into answering customer service calls. Neteller's customers didn't realize they were dealing with a one-man customer service department. "People would phone in and say, 'Gee, every time I call I get you,'" he recalls, laughing. He was also sorting out the bugs of the new system, a big part of his new job. Meanwhile, Lawrence still dealt with his various real estate developments, designing and building the back end of the Neteller business model. His friends agree it was probably the hardest Lefebvre had ever worked in his life. Lefebvre says it wasn't that hard because he always enjoyed the social aspect of work, and he spent almost all his time on the phone chatting with customers. But they were definitely the longest days he ever worked. "I think it helped that he was surrounded by these young guys, and I suspect they were toking and partying and joking around and having a good time," says Jane. "John doesn't groove on the work. He grooves on the people. He would make everybody feel good about themselves, and that's an important aspect of business. But actually dealing with the dollars and cents, that is not John."

Steve Glavine met Lefebvre in the late summer of 2001, when Neteller was just getting going. Glavine, out of university for four or five years by then, was looking for a career move. He was doing web design, but he wasn't good at it. He was a tech geek who wanted to create something. Lefebvre, having heard about him through a contact, was interested in Glavine, as he had some experience with Cold Fusion, a programming language that Neteller's website used. On a Friday afternoon he met with Lefebvre and Lawrence, and they told him the story of their exciting new payments business. Glavine knew nothing about online gambling and could see that the entrepreneurs were cash-strapped. They had hardly any employees in a huge warehouse space. But the next morning they called with a technical problem and asked if he could help. He went over to work and he went back the next day, and the day after that, and then he asked if they could come to an arrangement. They agreed, and after two weeks he submitted an invoice to Lefebvre. Lefebvre took a look at the invoice and said they couldn't afford to pay it. "But if you stay working for us, we'll hook you up down the road," he told him. Glavine had a good feeling about the opportunity, so he stayed, working for free, mostly with Lefebvre, the two of them pulling long days at the leased office space. Lefebvre worked in an empty room that was about a thousand square feet of space, and in the other giant, two-thousand-square-foot room was Glavine and Lawrence. When he needed rent money, they'd cut him a cheque for a couple of hundred. It was about six months before he drew a salary. "It was a bad time to start a dot-com," Glavine says. "The entire dot-com thing had blown up that year. It was imploding. If you went to a bank to ask for money to start one, they'd laugh in your face." Lefebvre was still driving the RAV4 and renting modest apartments, drinking cheap Chianti that came by the double-size jug. Glavine remembers that his boss had a bag of clothes and a guitar and that was about it. Lefebvre would come to work in surfer-brand T-shirts. For now, he had escaped the navy suits.

The work, says Lefebvre, was exhilarating. While he found aspects of law interesting enough, his favourite time working at a law office had always been his meetings with clients. He's a people person, and if the interaction is casual and fun, as opposed to buttoned up, so much the better. The new culture brought out a new work ethic for Lefebvre. His enthusiasm was infectious. The way he inspired others to get on board was similar to the way he won the presidency of the university student union. People just wanted to belong.

"It was just me and him in the office 90 per cent of the time," recalls Glavine. "I really got to know him and like him, and he's the reason I stayed and trusted them to continue on." When everything took off so quickly, it made sense to hire tech workers who could help Glavine. The problem was, there wasn't time to properly train anybody. Glavine's job was in Glavine's head, says Lefebvre. Nobody knew what he did. He was working twenty-hour days, sleeping four hours or less a night, and subsisting on coffee and Pepsi.

The space filled up. A couple more staffers were soon added, then a fifth and a sixth. Lefebvre, who was in his late forties, had found his groove. As the senior guy in the room, he could set the tone. There were no executives to report to, no meetings to attend. "All of a sudden it would be 11 o'clock in the morning and someone would yell 'Hacky sack!' and we'd kick around a hacky sack for fifteen minutes, and then get back to work," says Lefebvre. "It was like college. And all I had to do was sit and talk to people who phoned me from places like Nevada and New Jersey." There was camaraderie in those early days; they became tightknit friends, the misfits who couldn't handle the conventional corporate world. Word got out that there was this cutting-edge, fun start-up that was paying well and had an anti-corporate vibe. They had more people requesting jobs than they could keep up with. "All the people working were complete fuck-ups in normal life, with like tattoos and weird shit that would prevent them from getting real jobs," says Lefebvre. "And they had such a difficult time, you know, coming to terms with modern life, the way it had unfolded. And then they would come to Neteller, and they had prodigious talents. They would just work all hours because they finally found something they could devote their hearts to. It was awesome. They had nothing mainstream about them, and yet they were doing wonderful things for us. It was a cool atmosphere. It was very, very cool. It was fringe-y, and the gambling industry is very intriguing. The coolest guys in the world are gamblers."

Meranda Glesby, who was twenty at the time, had been referred through a friend for a customer service position at Neteller. "We were all excited for this new opportunity, even though we didn't know it would become as big as it became," she says. "We were young kids, and half of us were educated and the other half were just street smart." Glesby fell into the latter camp. "We never had opportunities to go to university or college because we were out on our own since age sixteen and working two or three jobs, and our parents were poor. So they really lucked out with the core group. And our jobs were always changing."

However, in order to grow, Neteller's founders had to do a couple of things. They had to fine-tune the security of its transactions, and they also had to go beyond Calgary and follow the money. They had to go where the gamblers were, and the online industries that catered to them. Lefebvre and Lawrence had to set up a second operation, and they knew exactly where. Lawrence and Natland had already been to the heart of gambling in Costa Rica, and Lawrence knew

Neteller would have to go too. By 2000, Lefebvre was living in San José with a few other staffers from the Calgary head-quarters, including Glesby. As the bookies and gamblers signed on for the service, Neteller's growth quickly acceler-ated. Online gaming blogs were all recommending Neteller as the go-to payments transfer service, better known as an e-bank or e-wallet. The future looked promising.

But was it legal?

THREE

Like Winning the Lottery

UNTIL THE ADVENT of Neteller, gamblers and bookies had relied on credit cards and wire transfer companies to move money between themselves and their customers, and had put up with the delays and fees that those services entailed. Neteller found a way to make life easier for them. Lefebvre and his team devised a virtual version of sliding one's chips toward the dealer to place a bet, and cashing those chips out at the cashier's cage. They'd created a platform, a software-based business, that if successful would connect potentially hundreds of millions of consumers to a service. Producers of platforms do not provide tangible services, like a plumber fixing your leaky faucet. Instead, they're the middlemen for those things, and they take a cut.

A platform is a way of connecting people on a large scale. In the old days, this might have been an auction house or a shopping mall. With the Internet, the scalability of it knows no limits, and the reach beyond bricks and mortar means you can pretty well make a platform business for anything. You might not feel comfortable if a stranger were to offer you a ride and ask for payment, but if there's a popular online ride-sharing platform for that service, people will get on board. You might not feel comfortable sleeping in a stranger's guest bedroom, but if there's a universal platform for that offering, you'll happily bed down. The creators behind the platforms often have no physical connection to the service provided: they don't own or maintain the cars, or own the homes or make the beds. Instead, they merely facilitate the exchange between the person providing the service and the consumer needing it. The best platforms make the exchange feel surprisingly easy and safe; because there is a review system in place, or safety features, or a high degree of familiarity, you feel you can trust them. You feel a sense of safety in numbers, even if the faces online are unseen and anonymous. And because these platforms scale up quickly and globally, the most successful facilitators have become billionaires. Proponents say the age of the Internet platform business is democratizing because it enables average people to make money with ease. Critics say these businesses arrive at such a lightning speed that policy makers and regulators can't keep up, and neither can a healthy level of competition. They create what some perceive as an unfair momentum that enables them to create billions of dollars in valuations, dominating the entire landscape. Others fear they are wiping out taxi unions and mom-and-pop retailers, and dismantling communities as homeowners choose lucrative vacationers over long-term renters, and storefronts close. In the case of Neteller, it was a platform that threatened the powerful American gambling industry, the banking industry and the government that collected taxes on the gambling industry.

Once Neteller got going, the money grew at a healthy pace, as if it had set into motion an unstoppable organism that was multiplying with a life force of its own. They early team members all felt that this thing had potential, and with each ringing phone, their hunch was paying off. A big reason for Neteller's rapid expansion was what they saw as a symbiotic relationship with PayPal, which had started at around the same time, in the late 1990s. That start-up had launched as a company called Confinity, which specialized in developing security software for handheld devices, but by 2000, with techie (and eventual billionaire) Elon Musk's involvement, it was focusing on the money transfer business. Confinity had merged with Musk's X.com online banking business and been renamed PayPal—and with that merger, the e-wallet concept was born. PayPal was offering the public the ease of electronic money transfers as an alternative to cheques, credit cards and wire transfers, and it turned out that there was huge demand for such a service. By 2002, it was offering shares to the public. eBay jumped at the offer, and for $1.5 billion, PayPal became a wholly owned subsidiary of eBay—which made sense, since most eBay customers were using PayPal for transactions.

In the fall of 2000, Neteller's IT innovator, Jeff Natland, used his personal PayPal account to process Neteller transactions. Neteller had been scrambling for several months, trying to figure out ways to enable gamblers to handily make their transfers, and which included awkward fiascos such as the Smart Card scheme, involving a "reader" device plugged into the computer and an app. Neteller would send the Smart Card package by Canada Post to each customer, who would then install the card onto their computer. It cost Neteller about $50 per customer, as well as the labour cost of having to take each customer through the process—Lefebvre spent many weeks on the phone guiding them through. In terms of cost, and customer satisfaction, it was a dismal failure. They also tried traditional Automated Clearing House (ACH) processing, which involves the customer giving bank authorization to transfer money directly from their bank account to Neteller's. It typically requires a form to be filled out, with the bank account, institution and routing numbers. Email money transfers didn't exist at that time.

And fraudsters were still eating up a lot of time and resources. Customers usually used Western Union or credit cards to make the payments to their Neteller accounts. Sometimes payments were made with a stolen credit card, and Neteller would be out of pocket. Neteller accountant Bob Edmunds remembers thinking that the company wasn't going to make it unless they could find a way to transfer money quickly and reliably without attracting fraudsters. Natland had figured out how to speed up the money transfers to de-risk the process even more. He saw that if he set up a PayPal account, their customers could just transfer the money to Neteller that way. Initially, the customer service team directed customers to use Natland's PayPal site. But eventually PayPal was added as a pay option on the company website, which meant customers had to have a PayPal account as well as a Neteller account. Lefebvre says that Neteller grew to become PayPal's biggest customer, with tens of millions of dollars in transactions flowing between the two. Best of all, Neteller paid only a small interest fee for the privilege, while its customers paid nothing.

You could make the argument that the relationship was less symbiotic than parasitic, which is the conclusion PayPal came to. The PayPal system had worked well enough that after a month or so, Neteller was able to pay its bills. IT guy Steve Glavine estimates that when he started in 2001, the company was pulling in about $6,000 a month in revenue. A month later, it grew to $30,000, and a month after that, it tripled. A month after that, it grew to $200,000. He says it was "mind-boggling to watch," and that "it went through the roof." Glavine had gone from making barely anything to earning about $50,000 a year, plus a 4 per cent share the partners gave him for his upfront work-for-free effort. At the beginning, of course, that didn't amount to much.

As the partners already knew, sports betting was particularly lucrative business. By the time football season began, the money really started to pour in, and things started to change for Lefebvre. His daughter, Emily, remembers her dad working eighteen-hour days; she hadn't seen this side of him before. Once Lefebvre had given up law, he dressed in jeans and T-shirts that had splotches on them, fully embracing his new dude role. While her mom had followed the straight and narrow, her dad was wild and carefree. Her friends thought she had the cool dad. She'd spend Tuesday nights and every other weekend with him at his various apartments, and once he started at Neteller, he'd come home for dinner, then apologize profusely because he had to go back to work. She thought to herself, "Okay, Dad, you've got yourself a desk job. That's... weird. But I think he saw the potential of it being a big deal." One day she got a call from him. "Emily, I'm in the black!" he told her excitedly. After years of struggle, he could finally pay off his debts. It was a momentous occasion. Emily never saw her father's financial burdens as a burden on her, though. "He was always around and taking care of me the best he could, even if he was in a lot of debt."

Meanwhile, staff at the San Jose, California, offices of PayPal couldn't figure out at first what was going on with the traffic surge on this Canadian account. Lefebvre says they began holding back a percentage of the transactions, similar to what credit card companies do with merchants in order to protect themselves against fraud. PayPal also began intermittently suspending the Neteller account, refusing transfers, which were as high as $70,000 a week. For Neteller, it was a painful blow. By that time, PayPal staff figured out Neteller's business and the fact it was piggybacking off the PayPal system. No doubt PayPal was questioning how much it was getting out of the deal. There'd been a few tense phone conversations, but this was a matter that needed to be dealt with face to face, e-wallet to e-wallet. Natland, Lefebvre and Lawrence flew to San Jose to have what they hoped would be a convivial chat with PayPal's operations team, to try to work out a deal that would suit everybody. Their goal was to stop the blocking of transfers.

The PayPal team was openly impressed to be meeting with the boy wonder Natland—somewhat famous in tech circles—whom they'd been dealing with over the last several months. Lefebvre remembers the staff buzzing when they realized that Natland was barely out of his teens. But then the Neteller team laid out their business model. Lefebvre being Lefebvre, he put it as delicately as he knew how. He proposed a way that Neteller could keep operating as it was, while effectively giving PayPal a cut. "We can give you access to this online gambling market without you guys having to get any gravy on your tie," he told them, nearly winking while he said it. He laid out the options. Neteller could use PayPal's service for a low fee but agree to exclusively use PayPal to make its transfers. And PayPal would promise not to compete with Neteller. Or, Neteller could pay a higher fee and use PayPal, but not exclusively. With this option, PayPal would again not compete for Neteller's gaming clients. Then there was the third option, which was they go to war as competitors, with Neteller stopping its use of PayPal. The PayPal team took in this information and said they'd think about it, says Lefebvre. But then,

after the Neteller men left the PayPal office, they knew that
PayPal would never go for their offer. He and Lawrence saw
that it would be easy for PayPal to take over a large share of
both Neteller's existing online gambling market and future
growth. "We decided war was inevitable, and it was only a
matter of when," says Lefebvre. "So that was it. We decided
in the car on the way back that we'd just go to war.

"And we quickly adjusted to working without the help
of PayPal, so we weren't dependent on their services come
football season in five months." PayPal swiftly grabbed the
bulk of Neteller's growth. For about a year, Neteller's client
base shrunk and it operated as a niche business. "It didn't
kill our business, but they were definitely eating our lunch,"
says Edmunds. "They were capitalized, and they had the
sales force and they could undercut us." Lefebvre says that
Neteller's existing customers showed a tremendous level
of loyalty, treating PayPal's overtures with disdain, even
when offered a sweeter deal. Things were chugging along
nicely for PayPal, whose customers were mostly shoppers
and others not involved in gambling. But gambling was an
extremely lucrative low-profile sideline for PayPal. "They
didn't talk about it much, but it made their bottom line look
multiples better," says Lefebvre.

However, when public company eBay came along, Lefebvre's lucrative little gambling business was starting to
look like a big liability. PayPal had caught the attention of
the attorney general of New York, Eliot Spitzer, who was
on a highly publicized mission to ferret out corruption on

Wall Street. Spitzer had an issue with PayPal acting as the go-between for American gamblers and offshore online casino operations. eBay was wary of getting in the attorney general's crosshairs, and it agreed to pull PayPal out of the online gambling business, but not for six months, according to Lefebvre. During that six months, PayPal made the most of its online gambling sideline, adding substantial revenue in the lead-up to the eBay deal. "And Spitzer goes, 'Fine,'" says Lefebvre.

But that didn't mean they were in the clear. By 2003, the U.S. Attorney's Office accused PayPal Inc. of violating the Federal Wire Act, and transmitting money for illegal gambling from October 2001 to November 2002. The company, now owned by eBay, agreed to a settlement of $10 million U.S.

"So they got out of the online gambling market, and Neteller filled that vacuum," says Edmunds. Edmunds had joined Neteller around the same time as Glavine, and both had a little less than 4 per cent stake in the company. He was a stay-at-home dad who had been running a small accountant business from home part time, charging an hourly rate for a regular list of clients. When he joined Neteller, he'd just wanted to find a start-up that held the promise of generating better returns. He didn't know a thing about the tech industry, but he sat next to Glavine, who told him what information he needed in order to keep the books. The gig economy wasn't going to secure his family's future, he thought at the time, but fortunately, his wife was a successful entrepreneur. He had just hoped for a $10,000 bonus for his efforts by the end of the year. "I was tied to an hourly rate, and I just wanted to do something with more upside. I was shutting down my practice and looking for something a little more lucrative."

Lefebvre was in Costa Rica when PayPal opted out of the online gambling market. His daughter, Emily, had gone off to university in Dublin, so his parenting duties were largely behind him. In Costa Rica, Neteller had established important bookie relationships. There, the industry was largely unregulated and dodgy, filled with sketchy characters who made a lot of money from gambling. These guys acted like big shots: they drove expensive cars, drank Cristal champagne and went everywhere with tanned, manicured women and a posse of tough guys with tattoos. Prostitutes were part of the casino scene, and crime was commonplace. Lefebvre was living in one half of a large duplex owned by his Costa Rican landlady, Cecilia, who had lived for several years in the U.S. The Neteller staff and anyone around could plainly see that Cecilia had caught his eye. She was an attractive fifty-seven-year-old and she lived in the other half of the duplex, separated from Lefebvre only by a wall. She was a vivacious and likable single mom who routinely helped the children of Costa Rica's slums. It was only a matter of time before the "hot" landlady and Lefebvre would begin a relationship.

The team rented office space and brought a few other Calgary staffers over, including Meranda Glesby, and they endured the challenges of doing business in a country where they didn't speak the language. Just to get a phone line for the office Lefebvre had to take a number and sit in a packed room and wait a whole day for his turn. It then took a month to get the phone installed. But it felt necessary to be there in San José, amid all the online gambling companies and bookies that could use their services. They were at the epicentre of online gambling, and it inspired confidence among the gambling companies that Neteller had a physical office where they could be contacted, face to face. For a time, Lefebvre loved the job, the place and the buzz that surrounded him.

"We would play poker all night and watch people do the crazy shit that they were doing. It was pretty bohemian," he says. "The way they do business down there, it's the Wild West, a free-for-all. The guys running the big gambling companies, some of them were good businessmen, but a lot of them were just hoods. They carried guns and had bodyguards with them—a bunch of *Scarface* types, but without the actual scars." He refers to the 1983 movie starring Al Pacino as a violent, drug-addled Miami drug lord. A more modern take on the money-fuelled bacchanal would be *The Wolf of Wall Street*, the Leonardo DiCaprio movie about a fraudulent broker intoxicated by his new-found lifestyle of excess.

With PayPal out of the way, Lefebvre soon realized that his little band of misfits from Canada had joined the ranks of Costa Rica's most exciting new online gambling entrepreneurs. "There was a tenfold increase in transactions—maybe a hundredfold," says Edmunds. "They went up massively once PayPal was out." Neteller had all sorts of side schemes too. At one point, Lawrence attempted to get into the porn business, says Lefebvre, providing those customers with the ease of the Neteller e-wallet. But another company had that market already cornered and made it abundantly clear to the upstarts that they should back off. Lefebvre says the office received an email with an image of the Neteller logo on a kiddie porn site. It was only a mock-up, an idle threat—but it still worked. "The message was loud and clear," he says.

If Neteller had been an experiment by a group that had nothing to lose, the lab beaker was now spilling over. But Neteller's growth made it inevitable that the company would have to start to act and function like a conventional corporate behemoth, particularly when it went public and became accountable to public shareholders, which was now the plan. Lawrence reached out to businessman Gord Herman, who understood the corporate world and knew something about dealing with booming new tech start-ups. Herman and Lefebvre had met several years before, when Jane's law firm was operating out of Herman's insurance agency space. Herman eventually sold the agency for millions of dollars, but he had his hand in several other successful ventures. He had been an executive at General Electric Capital, involved in leasing. And before Neteller, he had been brought in as chief executive officer for a high-tech incubator in Calgary that started at the same time as Neteller. There he worked for a young guy named Cameron Chell, who had gone from the family farm to a $3-billion tech business, with a personal fortune worth around half a billion dollars. Chell was too clever for his own good. He and his partners had created the precursor to what would become the cloud, an online software storage system, and they also ran a payments company similar to Neteller and PayPal. But it never took off. Chell had a dozen companies going and was "burning through $5 million a month of his cash," says Herman. Herman told him that he wanted it in writing that, with the declining capital, they would agree to shut down all companies but the two that were most viable. But Chell had a go-to-war attitude and insisted that all companies had to stay alive. Herman finally left, knowing that things were spiralling out of control. Chell had developed a drug habit and was disappearing all the time. The losses were mounting. Herman hung in there and tried to help him, but ultimately he started working nights at Neteller, where he quickly saw they were onto something.

As for Chell, he would eventually get clean, rebuild his life and start new businesses—and occasionally give talks opening for Tony Robbins. "He was a guy who could lose it and make it all over again," says Herman. "He's a scrambler, whereas Johnny is a totally different animal. 'Cavalier' is the proper term for Johnny. He had no use for money."

Herman, on the other hand, had come from humble beginnings and appreciated a new Mercedes and fine wine. He started as CEO of Neteller in September 2002, when the office was still operating with the same disorderly vibe of a campus newspaper. They were on track to make around $200,000 net that year, and everyone was happily employed, doing their thing, playing hacky sack and smoking pot on their breaks. "It was an eclectic group," he recalls. "There was Steve Lawrence, who's certainly not a corporate guy. They were a ragtag group of people making some cash flow, and making a little money off of it. They were having fun."

Lefebvre says he and Lawrence both knew early on that their strength was in coming up with the ideas, not executing them. "We knew from the beginning that, if it took off, we would need pros to run it. And to me, the whole point of getting rich was to *not* work. So we went with the smart money and turned it over to the pros."

Herman threw himself into the business, soon working eighty-hour weeks. "To me, it had an opportunity to compete against Western Union, to compete head on against the banks in foreign exchange and currency movement across borders. Gaming was a means to the end—the target was money transfer. To be clear, I am not a payments person. I didn't know a lot about it, but I had been involved in companies that had owed payment companies." The first thing Herman did was open everyone's eyes to the reality that Neteller was, essentially, a tech company—and for a tech company, it all comes down to security against fraud.

Herman made it his goal to figure out how to transfer money quickly and securely by determining a person's identity, which was key to Neteller's success. He saw the transfer in terms of a loan. If Neteller could safely identify someone as a credible client, it could effectively loan that person the money they needed for the two days it would take for the transfer to clear. That way, they could gamble freely without delay. The IT team came up with a way to identify a client by their computer address with their credit information. They acquired profile information from a large credit company and used the information to ask a potential client a series of questions to determine if they were honest. If that person began using Neteller and then tried to deny a transaction, it would be pretty tough considering it came from their computer. "They couldn't get up in the morning and say, 'That wasn't me that gambled that money,'" says Herman. "If they did, we would say, 'Well, it came from your laptop and using your passwords with all your bank information, so it had to be you,' and they would admit to it, and then we would shut them down." He had figured out a way to de-risk the transfers. "We had virtually no fraud. There was no such thing as a charge back anymore. So now we gave the merchants an opportunity to move away from credit cards, which also had hefty fees. Our fees were less. It was the perfect opportunity for Neteller to move into that market."

They named the two-day loan InstaCash and charged an interest of 8.9 per cent for two days. Calculated annually, that adds up to a rate of about 1,625 per cent says Lefebvre. "And yet the customers loved the convenience of it, so they paid the ridiculous rate quite happily." More than 60 per cent of their deposits became InstaCash deposits, and customers were lining up to pay them the absurdly high rate.

And the company didn't even need to advance any money for a loan. Behind the scenes, they were tongue-in-cheek, calling this lucrative bit of loan shark-style service "e-jack-u cash." ("Jacking" is street talk for stealing from someone.) By the next year, profits soared to around $25 million. Neteller went from twenty employees to three thousand within a couple of years. In terms of revenue, Neteller was leaving other dot.coms in the dust, including a start-up called Amazon.

Lefebvre's brother, Ted, remembers visiting the Neteller operation, which had expanded and moved to Edmonton Trail, a four-lane road in northeast Calgary flanked by low, flat-roofed cinder-block buildings grouped into drab strip malls with parking lots. Ted worked in the oil and gas industry that drove the Albertan economy, and he didn't see much of his brother. But he kept in touch, and when he heard about Lefebvre's booming new business, he dropped by to check it out. He walked up the stairs and saw about seventy young people working at computer stations, the place buzzing with phone conversations. Neteller was running three eight-hour customer service shifts around the clock. The energy of money making was in the air. Ted tells me that if his brother is the hippie of the family, then he's more of a cowboy. He has been known to don a pair of red cowboy boots while wearing shorts. At one time, Ted was a "landman," an oil-industry term for the person who approaches landowners and offers to buy the subsurface rights on behalf of major petroleum companies. He's retired now, but when he was working, Ted was on the executive committee of the sixteen-thousand-strong American Association of Professional Landmen, and he spent a lot of time with Texan oil guys. He was taken aback by his older brother's late-date success, and surprised that he would find his calling in gambling. "I tend to make up stories," he tells me, "but my understanding was, within the first year, they had six hundred off-track bookies signed up with Neteller, and it's those bookies that required their clients to have a Neteller account. Do the multiplier on that—and holy mack. You know?"

Things continued to move along pretty quickly. Herman took the company public. Once public, the team wanted to establish the company where online gambling was solidly legal, because in Canada it was neither legal nor illegal, and the banks in Canada were leery—"except National Bank, which got right away what we were doing and understood that it was no different from issuing a credit card, and then customers gambling with that—which *every* bank was doing," says Lefebvre. Online gambling was too new to have tested the legal system, and the Government of Canada to this day doesn't have any standing on it. The Americans couldn't be trusted: they had been grumbling about online gambling for a long time, no doubt eager to protect their own casino industry. Meanwhile, Britain has a long-established history of bookmaking, and so in October 2003, a year after he started, Herman moved the company to the Isle of Man—which was also a tax haven. The Isle of Man office had skeletal staff: the bulk of operations continued at the large Calgary office. "So the belief now is, we are taking money from U.S. citizens, moving it out of the U.S. to a legal online gaming company and we are in a legal jurisdiction," Herman says. The company went public a few months later, renaming itself Neteller PLC. The public was offered 15 million shares for purchase. Lawrence and Lefebvre continued to own 71 per cent of the company, and of that amount, Lawrence owned 65 per cent, Lefebvre 35 per cent. Not long after the Isle of Man office opened, Lefebvre stepped down from his role as president, but he stayed in Costa Rica.

Lawyers vetted the move to the Isle of Man, so they felt safe, operating as they were, from a jurisdiction where gambling was a long and storied tradition, and very legal. But wanting to be completely transparent with their public shareholders, as required by law, the Neteller executives added a clause in the prospectus that indicated there was uncertainty about the legality of online gambling in the U.S. In that way, they had covered themselves against any accusations that they failed to disclose anything about their business. They weren't the only new publicly limited company to include such a waiver in their prospectus. British online gambling company BetOnSports, founded by Gary Kaplan and run by David Carruthers, one of the biggest sites in the U.S., had also included the clause that its business was not necessarily legal in the U.S. "One of the beauties of moving to Isle of Man, we were the only Canadians there and we were living and working and breathing Neteller," says Herman. "All we talked about was business. It was a fun time. The company was booming."

Glesby had been the company's first paid employee at the Calgary office, working in customer service, and the company had brought her to Costa Rica because she was a fast learner who had a straight-talking ease with customers. She recalls Lefebvre attempting to play the corporate game, at least briefly. Lefebvre took his staff shopping at a strip mall when the company went public. He outfitted them in suits for a gaming industry convention in Toronto, with Herman and other executives. "John wanted to make sure his team was presentable," she says. "There were a lot of changes. That next year, we expanded and got better and bigger, but some people said, 'Screw this shit,' and they left." The company culture was transitioning from ragtag to corporate. In Calgary, there was no time for hacky sack. People who weren't getting with the new program were dismissed. This didn't sit well with Glavine, who quit. He didn't want to work in a corporate atmosphere, and he didn't need to. He had 4 per cent in the company, which would eventually allow him to cash out and retire by age thirty-two. "It went beyond my wildest dreams," he tells me.

Glavine hadn't been in it just for the money. "It changed for me, from a bunch of friends hanging out and doing something awesome and exciting to a job, and once that happened, I started to slowly lose interest." He asked for a six-month leave, and he delegated a few people to take over his IT responsibilities. The handover to the new IT team was a lot of work; in the end, it took 150 programmers to replace him. Lefebvre says that Neteller wouldn't have happened without him. He planned to come back, but after a couple of months he realized he had mentally checked out. By 2005, he was done with Neteller. The windfall had been made. Edmunds says, "It was like winning the lottery." Around that time, Glesby remembers Lefebvre being sidelined. The laidback, hippie management style was no longer needed, and Lefebvre too had grown bored with the business now that it had lost its start-up vibrancy. One person tells me off the record that he was spending more time on the tennis court than at work. Lefebvre says in actual fact he didn't spend any time at work. "That was the whole point," he says.

The business was ticking along without Lefebvre, though Glesby missed his input. Herman went to Costa Rica on Neteller business only once, for a meeting, which Lefebvre did not attend. It's not clear why, but it's likely he wasn't invited. "John is brilliant, but he's not a Wall Street guy," explains Herman. Glesby believes Lefebvre had an important role to play at times in the then-unregulated world of Costa Rican gambling. "In this industry there are certain types, and he had the right protocol, shall we call it. He knew what to say and what not to say kind of thing, whereas sometimes a guy in a suit going to a sports bookie is not going to close the deal. A hippie who just smoked a doobie is a little more chill and is on the same level as everybody else there, and it jived really well. It was good to have John, but on certain days, it was better to send someone else."

Lefebvre says Herman did change the culture, and he quite happily resigned his position as president. "Then I kept my distance, because I wanted it to be Gord's show," says Lefebvre. "The last thing a manager needs is people going around him to the owners." He had accomplished what he needed. Lefebvre remained as director of the public company, holding onto less than 26 per cent of remaining shares. He had become an incredibly wealthy man—worth about $350 million U.S., most of it in shares, but also a large chunk of it in cash. When I ask Lefebvre if he went out and celebrated his sudden wealth, he can't think of a particular night or event. He only remembers purchasing better cars. He had turned fifty, and although he'd enjoyed his share of partying, he says he couldn't relate to the twenty-four-hour, next-level party happening in Costa Rica. He stuck to his inner circle, and he even took a third crack at marriage, to the landlady. He purchased a seaside property in the coastal resort town of Manuel Antonio, with a plan to build an ultra-luxury home. Lefebvre brought Cecilia's adult sons on board and named the development an acronym of all their names. It was a new work project for Lefebvre: he wanted it to be the best residence on the Pacific Ocean.

His life had dramatically changed. He now flew between California and Costa Rica. He owned two beachfront houses in Malibu, one of them down the hill from Cher's house. The first house had been a meditative retreat, a place where he sat and played his grand piano, stoned and content, while taking in the endless ocean view. The other, more expensive house was to accommodate friends and family who visited. The Toyota had been replaced with rare sports cars and a BMW motorcycle. "He went from being a hippie to a rich hippie," says brother Ted. Lefebvre began to order the $900 bottles of wine he once scoffed at. He was on a first-name basis with the hostesses at Malibu celebrity hotspot Nobu, the guy who could book a table any time he wanted. "In those days, if I passed $1,000 lying on the ground, I probably wouldn't have bent over to pick it up," he says.

Not long after Neteller opened its Isle of Man office, it shut down operations in Costa Rica. Having resigned his position as president, Lefebvre gave up on Costa Rica too. His marriage to Cecilia had failed, and he was tired of living in a place where he didn't speak the language. As part of their settlement, Cecilia got the seaside development, and she eventually turned it into a successful resort. Seeking a quiet refuge, Lefebvre purchased properties on Salt Spring Island, the Canadian mecca for artists and people who make natural soap and grow organic produce. He divided his time between there and Malibu, in many ways the opposite of Salt Spring Island. But as a kid, he'd been captivated by his Beach Boys albums, and to be truly successful was to live a life of Californian surf. He purchased a private jet and a hangar, and he hired his own pilot. He'd fly wherever he wanted, whenever he wanted. If he wanted to see his daughter, Emily, in Dublin where she attended university, he'd just hop onto his plane. If, at the last minute, he wanted to take friends to the 2004 Olympics in Athens, that's exactly what he did. If he felt like flying his jet from Burbank to Santa Monica—about a half-hour drive by car—he did.

The only staffer who stayed behind in Costa Rica was Glesby. Outgoing and cheerful, she had married and started a family, and she loved her new life. Glesby didn't make the same money her peers had, but she says that's because she had negotiated a different deal. Glavine and others had worked upfront for free, whereas she couldn't afford to do that. She chose to get a paycheque instead of a percentage of the profits, but she did get bonus shares later on, and she wisely purchased several more on top of those. When she's at all regretful that she didn't request a percentage for herself in those early days, she quickly turns upbeat. "It's because of Neteller that I ended up in Costa Rica, and for that I'm grateful."

By 2006, Lefebvre had been out of the business for three years, living the high life. Meanwhile, unbeknownst to him, the U.S. had begun taking a much more aggressive position on online gambling. Herman, who had stepped aside as CEO and become chair of the board, sensed danger in the air. They were no longer operating in a grey zone. In July, the House of Representatives had passed legislation to come down hard on Internet gambling and any industry facilitating it. By October, Neteller's U.S. transactions would become illegal. Herman held a board meeting. "I said, 'We need to stop payments from the U.S. immediately. We are out of that business. And if we don't stop, I resign now.'" Because millions of dollars of American money was tied up in online gambling sites, the U.S. authorities said they wanted Neteller to wind down its operations over a period of several weeks, to give its U.S. customers time to get their money out. "So we agreed to do an orderly wind down of the company, to stop doing transactions by mid-January," says Herman. Because Lefebvre was no longer involved in the business, he wouldn't have been privy to the discussions. He was oblivious to danger, though his friends, including Jane, were warning him to stay away from the U.S. Other online gambling businessmen had been arrested months prior, including BetOnSports CEO David Carruthers, a Brit who'd worked in gambling his whole life. Carruthers had made it his passion project to legalize online sports gambling in the U.S. His company had keystone investors such as Morgan Stanley and Merrill Lynch, and its public stock was, like Neteller, sold on the London AIM stock market. His company had also started out in Costa Rica. Carruthers' is a cautionary tale.

In the summer of 2006, Carruthers was returning from a company meeting in the U.K., changing planes in Dallas on his way to Costa Rica. At the airport, he was met by U.S. federal agents and arrested on fraud charges. Carruthers and ten others, including BetOnSports founder Gary Kaplan, were named in the indictment by federal prosecutors, accused of taking bets from American citizens by phone and the Internet, and of failing to pay excise taxes. The company was forced to shutter the majority of its business, and Carruthers was removed from his position. Internet gambling stocks plummeted.

Carruthers spent nearly six years struggling against the U.S. legal system. He spent three and a half years under house arrest in St. Louis, without an income. After much back and forth, he reached a deal with the U.S. government:

he would admit to breaking its laws in return for thirty-three months in prison. He served only seventeen and a half because of good behaviour. Released at age fifty-five, it took him several years to rebuild. In Asia, he embarked on a career in the fashion industry. It didn't work out, but he learned Mandarin and eventually worked his way back into the online gambling industry, which is huge business in China. It was also by then a much safer climate for the online gambling sector than it had been in the early 2000s.

Neteller wouldn't escape the wrath of the United States Department of Justice, despite company executives having prudently begun the process of winding down their American operations. To many observers, it seemed that the Americans were protecting their bottom line under the guise of moral superiority. Whatever their motivation, they were getting increasingly aggressive and weren't about to turn a blind eye to a foreign company that had transferred billions of U.S. dollars offshore. Their aggression would change everything for the company. It would also change everything for Lefebvre.

FOUR

America Is Not Pleased

ON THE MORNING of Monday, January 15, 2007, Lefebvre was at his Malibu beach house and had just sat down with a cup of tea. He was thinking about a date he had the next night with a woman named Hilary Watson, from Salt Spring Island. The two had been dating for a few weeks, and Lefebvre had plans to fly back home to Salt Spring to see her. In Malibu, he'd been casually dating someone else, but with Hilary on the scene, he needed to figure out a way to deliver the news to the woman that he was no longer interested. Aside from his third marriage falling apart a couple of years prior, life had been smooth in the three years since he'd left Neteller. He lived in a house with ocean views from every room, a Bösendorfer grand piano, an expensive collection of wine, antique rugs and high-priced art. To some friends, it appeared that he was enthralled by his ability to buy what he wanted, but Lefebvre insists he never let that define him. "I was a grown-up kid in a candy store. I knew to have fun in it, but I was never owned by it."

It was a holiday Monday in the U.S., Martin Luther King Jr. Day. His doorbell rang, which was strange for so early in the day, never mind on a holiday. It rang again, and over the intercom a female voice said: "This is the FBI. You must come to the door immediately." Lefebvre's house was on a slope, and the main rooms were at beach level. He ascended the stairs to the front door and opened it. There stood two FBI agents and three U.S. marshals. After confirming his name and his involvement with Neteller, the FBI agent told him he was arrested on charges of money laundering, racketeering and conspiracy, and they turned him around and handcuffed him. They then led him back inside, down his spiral staircase and into his kitchen, where they seated him at the long wood kitchen table where he'd set down his tea moments before. Just then, Lefebvre's cell phone, which was lying on the table, buzzed. Lefebvre could see Steve Lawrence's name on the display. FBI agent Maryann Goldman said, "I'll take that," picked up the phone and answered it. The line went dead. Lefebvre experienced all the sensations of going into shock. He couldn't gather his thoughts, and he had the strange sensation that time had stopped, that he was suspended in the moment: "I couldn't focus if I tried, but things were also perfectly focused." This was the nightmare come true, and his mind kept turning to the L.A. jail cells and the cellmates who awaited him. "I kept thinking, 'Where am I going to be? What does this mean? Is this completely over now or what?' I remember thinking, 'Yeah, there's nothing you have to do but watch this unfold. Just be cool, and be peaceful. Be in the universe. No prison walls can confine a spirit as big as the universe.' But at the same time, I felt totally fucked. Maybe the only part of me that's busted is my ego, but unfortunately for this bodhisattva, my ego was still attached to my ass and it was going to a U.S. federal prison. They were threatening me with three twenty-year sentences, one each for conspiracy, racketeering, money laundering. They kept saying that this was such a massive criminal undertaking and it would make it easier on me if I helped them."

In the back of the squad car, he was allowed to call his counsel and business manager, Geoff Savage. Savage didn't answer, so Lefebvre called his assistant, Marian. He told her that he was seated in the back of a squad car with U.S. federal marshals and the FBI, and that he was under arrest and going downtown. He would not be home tomorrow, he told her. Meanwhile, Lefebvre's former Neteller partner Steve Lawrence had been arrested by the FBI and detained in the U.S. Virgin Islands in ankle chains. He had been arrested while travelling on a cruise ship that stopped at the U.S. Virgin Islands, on a warrant from the U.S. Attorney's Office in New York. He too was charged with money laundering and racketeering. The FBI had been monitoring the movements of Lefebvre and Lawrence for some time, trying to nab them when they were both on American soil. Lawrence lived in the Bahamas and had travelled to the U.S. several times in that last year. He had been on a cruise with his family when the ship made an unscheduled stop at St. John, one of the three Virgin Islands and which is part of the U.S. When Lawrence and his family disembarked, the FBI agents were waiting for him. At that time, the FBI knew that Lefebvre was at his house in Malibu. Their plan to catch both men simultaneously had been realized.

Lefebvre has a fantasy of alternate events that unfolded that day. It's the sort of fantasy you play out in your mind when you've stepped into a lousy situation—one that would never happen. But it feels good. Instead of answering his doorbell, he sees himself just coming home on his BMW GS 1200 motorcycle, wearing a full-face helmet, and just continuing on, casually riding by the FBI agents at his door and then riding for hours, east past Joshua Tree, heading away from Vancouver or Calgary for a quiet border crossing through, say, Minnesota or the Dakotas and then westward to his home on Salt Spring—where he hunkers down and deals with the American offensive behind the hopefully protective wall of Canadian citizenship.

He wasn't entirely reckless when he was spending time stateside while businesspeople in the gambling industry were being arrested. Steve Lawrence and others, including Gord Herman, had also believed they were safe to travel to the U.S. After all, Neteller wasn't an online gambling company per se, it was just doing what every bank was doing with credit cards, what Western Union and FedEx were doing with their processes, and besides, it was in the process of pulling out of the U.S. market and complying with the new Unlawful Internet Gambling Enforcement Act that came into effect on October 13, 2006. The act transformed the industry by prohibiting gambling businesses "from knowingly accepting payments in connection with the participation of another person in a bet or wager that involves the use of the Internet and that is unlawful under any federal or state law," according to a state regulator document. The Federal Wire Act had not prohibited Internet gambling, whereas this new law did. It was a game changer, particularly for companies listed on the London Stock Exchange that had been taking American payments. In its wake Herman had ensured that the company was no longer involved in American transactions.

By afternoon, Lefebvre had been taken to the Metropolitan Detention Center, a federal prison in downtown Los Angeles, where he was booked and assigned a cell with another inmate. He soon learned that the man was German and had stolen cigarettes from a car. The room smelled of rot because the man made his own version of yogurt. He soured small cartons of milk from the cafeteria by leaving them on the heater in the cell for days to let curdle. He also brought iceberg lettuce back to the cell, mixing the "yogurt" with vinegar to make salad dressing. As the man talked, his mouth full of food, Lefebvre felt his stomach heave. The cell had two bunk beds, a toilet and a sink. Lefebvre quickly learned cellmate etiquette. If one of the men had to use the toilet, the other lay on his bunk facing the wall. Lefebvre feared that he might lose his mind. The feeling of confinement was overwhelming. "I was completely surrounded with people looking at five and ten and fifteen years. I was among them in the sense that, as far as I knew at the time, I was possibly looking at something really serious. But I also knew how the law works ... so I was able to convince myself not to get too carried away with jumping to exaggerated conclusions. But your every impulse is to do just that."

In the prison's common area, he found books to read, which helped him get his mind off his situation. Two days later, Lefebvre had a bail hearing. Herman had found a Beverly Hills lawyer, Vince Marella, to represent him. Marella wore the most exquisitely constructed suits Lefebvre had ever seen. At the hearing, Marella, wearing one of his best Italian suits, offered a bail bond of $5 million. When word got back to the prisoners about the bond amount, Lefebvre's status was instantly elevated. Who was this older white guy? The other prisoners stared his way, circled around a little closer and asked his advice on various legal matters, for which he had no answers. Meanwhile, Lefebvre still needed to produce the $5 million U.S. The promise to deliver had been made, but the money wasn't yet in Marella's hands. Jane took it upon herself to get the funds necessary for her friend's bail. She'd been overseeing Lefebvre's finances, so she had access to his accounts. But word of his arrest had reached Canadian media and his face was on the front pages. In the *Globe and Mail*, his picture with his mother at a Dalai Lama event in Vancouver appeared above the fold under headlines that read "money laundering." The bank wouldn't release the funds because it was uneasy about the implications of the American money laundering charges. Jane was apoplectic. "I stormed over to the bank, along with Murray Pettem for moral support," she says, "and we pounded our fists on the table, and told them they were acting inappropriately and these were funds from publicly traded shares, not laundered money." The bank had no legal standing, so it relented and agreed to forward the money to Marella's law firm.

Early on Thursday morning, a guard awakened Lefebvre and told him that he was being shipped out. Lefebvre asked if the bail money had come through, but the guard didn't know. The only information he had was that Lefebvre was being moved to another jail—in Oklahoma City. Along with several other prisoners, Lefebvre was put in handcuffs with arm shackles and leg irons, then loaded onto a bus. It was a special bus, with bars separating the occupants into three sections—for guards, male inmates and female inmates. Chained to their seats, they were driven to a government airport at the small city of Victorville, in San Bernardino County, California. There, they waited on the tarmac for hours while many busloads of other prisoners from South California jails arrived. When there were a couple of hundred prisoners assembled, they boarded the airplane, nicknamed Con Air. Their plane was different from a commercial jet. It was all white, with no other markings except for a registration number on its side. Lefebvre thought about being in an airplane with chains around his feet and wrists. He broke out in a sweat. How would he escape if there were a crash? The flight attendant, a U.S. marshal, only told them: "In the event of an emergency, follow instructions."

Mid-afternoon, while Lefebvre was in the air, Vince Marella arrived at the L.A. Metropolitan Detention Center. But of course, Lefebvre was not there, and nobody could say where he'd gone. Marella, a seasoned lawyer, was shocked. Jane got a call. "Vince said, 'You could have pushed me over with a feather.'"

By Friday morning he had learned that his client had been transferred to the Oklahoma City Federal Transfer Center, a major processing hub where prisoners are held and sorted and transported on to other jurisdictions. In Lefebvre's case, the undercover gambling transactions over a computer had occurred in New York, so the district attorney in New York was pursuing the charges. The Federal Wire Act had been used a few years earlier to charge William Paul Scott of WorldWide Telesports Inc. in Antigua. Scott had to pay $6.9 million in civil forfeiture. It was the same year that PayPal and eBay forfeited $10 million. In 2001, Jay Cohen was arrested for the same charges for his gambling company WSEX out of Antigua. He was sentenced to twenty-one months.

In Oklahoma City, Lefebvre lay awake in his cell wondering what crime his new cellmate committed, and he tried to concentrate on holding it together. By Sunday, a guard came to collect Lefebvre from his cell. Marella had arrived to spring him free. Lefebvre was elated.

"I wish I had friends like yours," the guard told him.

"What does that mean?" Lefebvre asked.

"Your friends came up with $5 million in bail to get you out."

Lefebvre smiled. "I don't have any friends. That money is mine!"

The guards gave him ugly street clothes, a cheap golf shirt, jeans, and a beige windbreaker. "How do I look?" he asked his lawyer.

"Like you just got out of jail."

Once on board their flight back to Los Angeles, the two men celebrated his release with champagne. But Lefebvre was thinking about the stash of pot he had back home. Once at the Malibu house, rattled and paranoid, he frantically opened every drawer until he found the pot and flushed it. Two days later, Lefebvre was back on a plane, heading to the Southern District Court in Manhattan, where he was to be arraigned. He would also submit to his first urine test. Marella planned to enter a plea of not guilty.

Lefebvre's former business partner Steve Lawrence had been arraigned the previous Friday. The two men were advised by their lawyers not to communicate, so Lefebvre didn't know anything about Lawrence's situation. Later, Lefebvre learned the details. Lawrence's lawyer had argued that the illegality of money transfers for gambling purposes was an untested allegation. None of those who'd

been arrested earlier went to trial but had merely plea-
bargained. As well, his lawyer argued that Lawrence had
been fully cooperative and voluntarily appeared in New
York, and had already paid $4 million of his bail. Lawrence
also had many ties to the U.S., with a New York property in
the Meatpacking District, and business connections to that
city. But it came up in Lawrence's hearing that as soon as he
had been arrested, someone had phoned Lefebvre; the FBI
agents believed that a Neteller colleague had been trying
to tip off Lefebvre so he could run for it. On that basis, U.S.
Assistant Attorney Timothy Treanor argued that the men
were a flight risk. He brought up the case of BetOnSports'
David Carruthers, who served three years of house arrest in
St. Louis. Treanor asked the judge to consider giving Lawrence a similar pretrial restriction. The judge decided that
Lawrence was restricted to New York until the end of February, after which he would be allowed to travel within the U.S.

When you have been smoking pot practically every day
for a lifetime, it can take several months for THC to entirely
leave your system. When the courthouse staff tested Lefebvre's urine, the testing official found enough THC in his
system to ask "Do you need to sit down?" Lefebvre got a
different judge from the one who presided over Lawrence's
hearing. Lefebvre's judge decided that Lefebvre's pretrial
travel was to be restricted to southern and eastern districts
of New York and the southern district of California. He
would be forced to surrender travel documents and obey
strict pretrial supervision. Because of his failed urine test,

he'd also have to undergo regular urine testing for drugs. If there were traces of THC in his urine, he'd have breached parole and broken the law again, which would be disastrous for him. The testing would be a tough part of the deal for Lefebvre, who'd been frequently using a particularly strong strain of pot. At first the tests were weekly, but eventually they would become monthly.

The days ahead weren't easy for Lefebvre, who knew he was looking again at serious jail time, potentially many years. The brief time he'd spent in a jail cell in Los Angeles and then Oklahoma City had traumatized him: "You don't know if you are going to keep your shit, because you are in this tiny room with somebody you don't know or care about that much, and you are completely without power, completely emasculated. I remember there were times I was lying in my bunk thinking, 'I don't know if I can make it through the night,' like I was going to bust out screaming.'"

As far as tragic flaws go, Lefebvre's would be his complete unwillingness to listen to sound advice from those he respected. When his mind is made up, it is made up. For many months before he was arrested, Jane had been strongly advising Lefebvre to avoid the U.S. Lefebvre thought she was being absurdly cautious. "He said, 'You're being ridiculous. They don't want me.'" One time, she got a call from him when he was in Malibu and he said, "Jane, they've arrested me! They've got me in manacles!" And then he started laughing. When the arrest was real, she didn't get a call from Lefebvre but from Gord Herman, who was at home in the Bahamas. He had emailed Jane with the news about Lawrence nine hours earlier, but she hadn't received the email. "I think the feds held it back so they could arrest them at the same time," she says. Herman then called to tell her that Lawrence had been arrested, and he told her to tell Lefebvre not to go to the U.S. But Herman didn't realize that Lefebvre was already there, at his Malibu house. "I was very upset, and very concerned, because I didn't think the U.S. would be kind to him," says Jane.

News of his arrest hit his former business colleagues hard. They didn't dare enter the U.S. and visit their friend because they too could easily be on the FBI's wanted list. To this day, some of them are reluctant to cross the border. So that they could help manage his money while he travelled the world, Lefebvre's money manager and friend, lawyer Geoff Savage, as well as his wife, were listed on joint bank accounts with Lefebvre—so they were terrified that they would be implicated in the money laundering charges. "I was living a nightmare for sure," recalls Savage. "I wouldn't go near the United States."

Glavine was at his Calgary home when he heard the news. "I was shocked, and concerned for my friends. The lawyers got in touch pretty quickly and said, 'Don't contact them, stay out of the U.S.' I didn't go down for another six years, but one time I went to see a buddy play in a baseball game in Washington, and when I crossed the border I was crapping my pants."

Bob Edmunds had retired from the company as its CFO by the end of 2005, but he remained on the board as a director. He was in Costa Rica when he heard about the arrests, and he too was concerned about how far the arm of the law would extend. Lefebvre's daughter, Emily, was about to make dinner for a friend when she got a call from Geoff Savage, telling her that her father had been arrested for money laundering. "I felt it in the pit of my stomach. That was brutal."

Lefebvre worried for the crews he'd hired to build his luxury Stonehouse guesthouse resort. It was a huge financial commitment, costing millions of dollars and employing more than a hundred tradespeople. He'd even hired an artist to bring in giant stones and create the version of Stonehenge that stands in the field overlooking the harbour. When word got out that he'd been arrested, the crews feared for their jobs and their unpaid hours. Hilary, who is now Lefebvre's wife, says it struck her that his biggest fear at the time was that people would be out of jobs because of his arrest. But Lefebvre didn't deal with their worry. Savage says that because Lefebvre was stuck in the U.S., he was left to handle the impacts. "Thank God John was in jail, because he didn't have to face the 101 supplicants who are wondering if it is the end of the world for them," says Savage. "We stickhandled that one."

Media response to the arrests was understandably in Lefebvre's favour. He hadn't absconded with anyone's life savings or pulled some scam on unsuspecting elderly people. He knowingly operated within the grey zone of American legislation that made little sense. His publicly traded business had been physically located outside the U.S., in a jurisdiction where online gambling was clearly legal. Adult Americans had made use of his service in order to gamble online, and it had served them well, and the company had taken every precaution to protect its customers against fraud. Edmunds says Neteller ran a conservative business, never overextending itself and always ensuring it had the cash on hand if it needed to pay people out. That fiscally conservative approach served the company well, because about 90 per cent of its customers were American. When the U.S. government shut Neteller down and said it would have to pay out the U.S. customers, the money was on hand to do that. "If we didn't have the money on hand, we could have been going down for fraud," Edmunds says.

American lawmakers couldn't claim a puritanical judgment over the Neteller service because at the time gambling was legally operated by the states themselves with the exception of two, Utah and Hawaii. And in two others— New Jersey and Nevada—it was legal for everyone who was licensed by the state. The only parties that would have been unhappy with Neteller were the American gambling industries and associated industries (such as hotels)— what Lefebvre calls the "hotel lobby"—losing out on the profits, and the American government losing out on tax dollars. The *Globe and Mail* published opinion pieces on the charges against the company, noting that Neteller's market value plunged from $3 billion the year before to $486 million. (Lefebvre regretted not selling his shares and tucking them safely into an offshore account, as the others had.)

The newspaper cited BetOnSports founder Gary Kaplan and CEO David Carruthers' arrests, and the fear that had been spreading throughout the industry as a result. It also underscored the hypocrisy of a nation so obviously quashing foreign businesses it found threatening to its own interests: "The U.S. crackdown on Internet gambling, a crusade that seems to involve arresting law-abiding citizens of other countries and threatening them with long prison terms, continues to claim new victims... While the U.S. authorities would like to paint [Lefebvre and Lawrence] as criminal masterminds, the fact is that they have broken no laws in either Canada or Britain, where their company is based. Instead, they have run afoul of the hypocritical U.S. desire to restrict gambling on the Internet while allowing it to flourish at home, where it produces billions of dollars in tourism and tax revenue," reads the editorial dated January 19, 2007.

In academic circles, Patrick Basham, who has a PhD in political science, is perhaps the most outspoken proponent of gambling. He is founding director of Washington, D.C.-based public policy research organization, the Democracy Institute, and is a controversial figure who is regularly quoted by media. The group's mission statement includes challenging conventional wisdom, stimulating policy debate and enlightening the public conversation. On American gambling laws relating to foreign businesses, few would argue with him. The libertarian penned a 2017 report called *Do As I Say, Not As I Do*, in which he lambastes the American attacks on "responsible, regulated online gambling" in

Antigua and Barbuda, and the prosecutions of Canadians such as Bodog's Calvin Ayre, "in order to ensure the successful application of ill-conceived domestic legislation." He accuses the U.S. of "myopic self-interest" over values such as the rule of law. In a nutshell, the U.S., he says, was engaged in a bullying campaign to prosecute foreign businesspeople in order to promote their own domestic interests—an act of protectionism by abuse of the criminal justice system. Lefebvre wholeheartedly agrees with Basham. Lefebvre says: "It is an utter abuse of the criminal authority that we entrust to government when it is used for no better purpose than hoarding the benefits of an industry to themselves."

At the same time, Lefebvre quickly understood that if he had been targeted by an unjust system, there were others in far worse situations. When he was in jail in Oklahoma City, Lefebvre met a fellow inmate at the Con Air waiting cells who was well into a forty-year term for dealing many pounds of marijuana. Unlike the overwhelming majority of inmates, who were men of colour, he was white. "It's comparatively rare for white guys to get thrown in American jail," says Lefebvre. He notes the hypocrisy of jailing a person for dealing a substance that has since become just another consumer good. Today, pot dealers who served time would be considered savvy entrepreneurs, part of a growing industry. But for decades before the recent legalization of marijuana, America was on a mission to jail drug dealers, including those who sold pot. As a consequence, hundreds of pot dealers, mostly African-American and Hispanic, were convicted and given sentences longer than terms served by some murderers. According to the Clemency Report, a project by journalist Dennis Cauchon, fifty-four people, some of them small-time repeat dealers, were sentenced to life without parole between 1996 and 2014 by federal judges for marijuana-related offences because of the "three strikes" provisions: commit a third federal felony and it's an automatic life sentence. Before leaving office in 2016, President Barack Obama issued pardons or reduced sentences for many people who had been serving time because of harsh anti-drug laws. But there are still many in jail for marijuana-related offences. According to the non-profit group Drug Policy Alliance, 608,775 Americans were charged with marijuana possession in 2018.

In Canada, where cannabis is now legal, there's a rough estimate that 250,000 citizens have possession-of-marijuana records haunting them. Lefebvre questions why marijuana use would even be an issue when a person is arrested. He feels it might be a case of the authorities simply taking the easy route to incarceration. "Once they find out you're on drugs, they pretty much don't have to do more investigating. They can say, 'You're in here because you are on drugs.' That's why they test your urine. The drug laws are making it so that the cops and prosecutors can go for doughnuts rather than fulfill their duties by prosecuting the case, then lamely forcing a 'plea bargain' with an inmate that breached a pot test."

IN THE FIRST eighteen months out on bail, Lefebvre wasn't allowed to leave California, and although the sun shone relentlessly, he was brooding. In the morning, he'd wake up with a racing heart. No amount of surf or beautiful people set to a Beach Boys soundtrack could lift him out from under the dark cloud of incarceration. He loved the weekly rides on his motorcycle through Los Angeles' notorious smog and freeway congestion but despised the destination: urine tests at the L.A. federal court house.

"I hope he doesn't mind me saying this, but I feel like that was his 'asshole phase,' after the arrest," Emily tells me. We're seated in a coffee shop on the east side of Vancouver, and she's just come from teaching a yoga class. She lives in a house nearby, with her husband, Padraig O Cinneide, a software engineer, and their four-year-old daughter, Ida. If her father was acting like an asshole at the time, it was understandable, she says, because he was living in a state of suspended terror, not knowing his fate and not knowing what information the FBI could use against him. He was uncharacteristically sharp-tongued and irritable. She remembers listening to his plan to tell off the judge who would be sentencing him. "He wanted to tell the judge what was on his mind when he went in for sentencing, and he was going to say, 'You fucking hypocrites, the system is rigged, blah blah.' I said, 'Okay, that's cool but think about Grandma, and Hilary and me, we don't want to see you put away. It will not end well. There is a time and a place, Dad, so maybe after you serve your time you can shoot your face off, but not in front of a federal court judge.'" When I asked Lefebvre about this, he said, "People who really love me give me shit when it's called for. Emily demonstrated to me wisdom and invited me to either accept it or go ahead and be about as bright as Homer Simpson."

In the meantime, what's a man in Malibu-exiled limbo to do but make a record with some of the world's best musicians? The summer that followed his arrest, Lefebvre embarked on a proper double album of the many songs he'd written over the years, and he wanted to use the best musicians who he could interest. The plan to make the record had originally been to record it in Vancouver, but because he was on "a leash," Lefebvre had no choice but to make the album in Los Angeles. Without the backing of a record label, he'd be funding the project himself. There wouldn't be any promotion or distribution, so he knew that the likelihood of a broad audience was low. He didn't care. He wanted to make the album that had been playing inside his head since he wrote those songs in the late 1990s, when he was busking for commuters.

Lefebvre, in 2005, told Canadian producer and musician Danny Patton about his plan, and Patton connected him with producer Brian Ahern, who was based in Nashville. Ahern, a fellow Canadian, is famous for recordings made with Anne Murray, Emmylou Harris, Johnny Cash, Roy Orbison, Willie Nelson and other country music icons. Lefebvre describes his style of music with a question: "What style is the Beatles' White Album?" Although new to the songwriting process, he is comfortable sliding between rock and country territory, and he enjoys the grand drama of orchestral arrangements. He occasionally delves into a ballad like Dusty Springfield's *All I See Is You*. Ahern could pull together a super group of studio musicians to give Lefebvre's songs a suitably professional lustre. Once Lefebvre knew he couldn't leave central California, it was natural to record the album in Los Angeles, the base for many of the world's most successful and experienced session players.

They settled on the famous Village Studios (formerly the Village Recorder) in West Los Angeles, off Santa Monica Boulevard, and Ahern booked a studio there for four weeks. They then set to work finding out who was interested and available. They visited legendary producer, songwriter and guitarist T Bone Burnett at his house in the L.A. neighbourhood of Brentwood, and he listened to one of Lefebvre's demos. "T Bone said, 'This stuff sounds pretty good already,'" Lefebvre recalls. "T Bone had a marvellous ease and made me feel right at home. He made us coffee and we sat to listen in the solarium off his kitchen." Burnett advised them to get Jim Keltner on drums, and said if they could do that, then all the other players would fall into place. Lefebvre says that's because Keltner is considered one of the best session drummers in the world. Luckily, Keltner had some time, so Lefebvre and Ahern invited musicians whose homes had Grammy Awards decorating the mantles, whose names graced the pages of music trade magazines, and who had played over the decades alongside all manner of music giants. There was keyboardist and guitarist Al Kooper, most famous for his studio work with Bob Dylan. Also among them was guitarist Greg Leisz, who'd played for the likes of Joni Mitchell, the Eagles and John Fogerty, and keyboardist Matt Rollings, who'd played with Lyle Lovett and Mark Knopfler. There was guitarist Dean Parks, famous for playing with Steely Dan and Michael Jackson, and keyboardist Patrick Warren, who'd played with guys like Tom Waits. Bonnie Raitt's bass player James "Hutch" Hutchinson joined the project. Glen D. Hardin, who had played piano and did band arrangements for Elvis Presley, worked with Lefebvre to draw the song charts the players would use. Jeff Greenberg, the owner of Village Studios, nicknamed the assembled band the "A Team" and told Lefebvre that it was an honour to have them all back in the studio.

Lefebvre was elated that they all agreed to the job, but he knew that even top-shelf session musicians had spare time and appreciated the income. The same went for Ahern. Not every gig is going to lead to a Grammy. But Lefebvre believed too that they weren't purely doing it for the money, that they appreciated the songs. "You can kick in the doors with money, but you can't stay in for long unless there is something of merit going on. Guys at that level do not want their names on just anything. They are lending their reputations to the work, and I am immensely grateful that they did. They wouldn't have stuck around if the songs were shitty, or if I was just another vain and annoying prima donna. They'd played for them all, and they could see that type a mile away."

Lefebvre says he despises coming off as a fan. He isn't the type to go backstage and hang out with Neil Young, though he had once been asked by some people to do just that. "If I were him and had just finished working that hard, I'd be more annoyed by the attention and would prefer the privacy."

Those days just before going into the studio, he was feeling self-conscious. Ahern told him, "John, these guys just want to be treated like normal people. They're willing to treat you as one of them. Don't act like a fan. Be who you are."

Lefebvre first met the musicians he'd hired on day one in the studio. Hardin had a couple of dozen songs charted out so that everybody could easily read their part. Ahern, a big man, wore cowboy boots with shorts, and he brought a blender so he could make protein shakes. Doughnuts and coffee were laid out for the musicians. Lefebvre entered the room, sat down and picked up his guitar as the veteran players quietly nodded to each other and assembled around him. As they continued to sit in silence, he realized they were waiting for him to start. "I was supposed to perform the song solo so they could watch it go by on the chart. It took me awhile to get used to that. I had only played in basements and at small gigs with friends. Now I was letting it all hang out for the best players in rock." By the end of the first run-through of a song that Lefebvre had written, Leisz said, "That was pretty good. How many more of those have you got?" Lefebvre was more at ease. He could almost relax. He played two songs for them that day, one on acoustic guitar at noon, the other on piano that evening, singing while the group followed along, listening closely until they picked it up. "Then they all just fiddled with it, each to themselves. They sounded like an orchestra tuning up. Then, after about fifteen minutes, it was one, two, three, four and they just played it. Astonishingly wonderfully." They continued on until around five o'clock, when they took a break for a catered dinner, then they worked on the second song until around nine or ten. They came in the next day for the noon call time and went through two new songs, and to Lefebvre's relief, they seemed to be enjoying them too.

"One of the things the A Team really appreciated was that Brian had us set up so we could play live together, old school. Studios usually don't do that anymore for economic and technical reasons. If I was playing piano or acoustic guitar, my mikes would pick up all the other players' stuff too—for example, if I made a mistake, they would all have to do it over. Brian solved those problems by putting noisy speakers in sound isolation, miking them there and then everybody listened back on headphones. So we could play live and, at the same time, talk to each other at normal levels. It was live magic and all the players really missed that traditional setup. For me it wasn't building the dream, it was actually living it."

Lefebvre played piano on about a third of the songs, seated in an isolation booth. He recalls the work as one of the best times in his life. Kooper, the most notorious of the group, spent eight days at the studio. Lefebvre noticed how the other musicians deferred to him. Once they got to know Lefebvre a little, the players asked him questions. "They asked me why I was doing it," he says. "I said that it seemed to me that the songs were good and I thought they deserved the treatment. I didn't have many illusions. The value of all recorded music had tanked because of Napster, and this wasn't the type of music that was still selling at all in those days. But it was the kind these players had all been playing for forty years." As he listened to the raw takes, he felt his nerves dissipate. Every Friday morning, he rode his motorcycle to the federal courthouse in downtown Los Angeles to do his urine test before going to the studio. For the first time in a long time, he had the routine of a daily job. For the first time in his life, he says, it was a job he loved.

Around the time they began mixing the album, in July of 2007, Lefebvre's lawyers negotiated a plea bargain. Knowing the way it goes with plea bargains, Lefebvre knew that things could go way worse for him if he insisted on his innocence. So standing before Judge P. Kevin Castel in the Manhattan courtroom, he pled guilty. With his lawyers by his side, he waived his right to be tried before a grand jury and his right to presumption of innocence. He waived his right to appeal and agreed that he was guilty of participating in a conspiracy from June 1999 to January 2007, of engaging in betting and wagering unlawfully, even though Neteller was never a gambling business. He also pled guilty to the charge, as read by Judge Castel: using a "wire communication facility for the transmission in interstate and foreign commerce of bets, wagers and information assisting in the placing of bets and wagers on sporting events," which entitled the recipient to receive money and credit. He was told that the maximum he could receive was five years in prison. As part of his guilty plea, he was also to forfeit $40 million U.S. Upon his lawyer's advice, Lefebvre admitted to the judge that his business of providing payment services to online gambling businesses serving American customers was wrong. But inwardly, he felt humiliated and angry that he was being forced into kowtowing to a law that seemed less interested in protecting citizens and more interested in protecting the bottom line of a powerful American industry. "My feelings tended toward being angry more than fearful, because I did consider it to be an injustice. They get to run gambling because they are the authorities, and I don't. For them it's good tax policy, and for me it's pernicious vice."

While Lefebvre awaited sentencing, the FBI conducted several interviews with him, trying to ascertain what he knew. From the outside, his life would have looked pretty serene: a man reading books on the beach, heading off on his motorcycle into the Santa Monica Mountains north of Malibu or into Joshua Tree in the desert north of Palm Springs. There were still dinners at Nobu, and by then Lefebvre had acquired a small collection of rhinestone-covered suits designed by the highly respected Manuel Cuevas. For many years, Cuevas had worked closely with legendary tailor Nudie Cohn. Cohn famously designed Elvis Presley's gold lamé suit and Gram Parsons' outlandish two-piece number festooned with marijuana leaves and poppy flowers that he'd worn on the cover of the Flying Burrito Brothers debut album. Lefebvre got three Cuevas suits from his Nashville shop, wearing them to concerts and the occasional party. He wore one to his daughter Emily's wedding too, without raising eyebrows. Her friends already knew about her eccentric dad.

His exile in Malibu went on for a couple of years before the United States Department of Justice decided he wasn't a flight risk and allowed him to visit Canada, in 2009. He wouldn't be allowed to contact any Neteller employees, who'd been advised to keep their distance from the cofounders. "They weren't allowed to tell me what they were telling the cops about me. But I had nothing to hide. How could we hide anything? We were a public company." Lefebvre hadn't had much to do with Neteller operations since the end of 2004 anyway. His only contact had been with the original shareholders and, other than Lawrence, he was still in touch with those guys. Herman resigned from the board soon after the arrests, and he had stayed in touch.

Lefebvre says the music sustained him through those dark days. "I had to come to terms with the idea that staying awake until four in the morning wouldn't solve my problems. I needed to get to sleep. Most thoughts, particularly at 3 a.m., are uninvited guests. But still, it so happens that some uninvited guests are treasures, like creative ideas."

Those sleepless nights ended up producing seven new songs during the making of the album. He liked the recording process so much that he made a second double album, in 2009, at Ocean Way Studio in Hollywood, with several of the same players, but this time including Little Feat keyboardist Bill Payne. The second time around, Lefebvre was more professional, he says, and the songs, including nine new ones, were less derivative. But he was never completely satisfied with the mixing. He thought it sounded flat compared with the way it sounded live, so he had the songs remixed. The two albums cost him more than half a million dollars U.S. to make, not including the remixes.

Lefebvre doesn't offer a lot of insight into why he wanted to make the albums other than that he considered the songs to be worth it and he wanted to record them with the best musicians available to him. He never really shopped the albums. He explains: "If Elvis Costello can't sell any records, why would I waste the effort?" A Canadian senator, an acquaintance, thought they were good enough to be heard, so he sent the recording to music manager Bruce Allen, whose clients include Michael Bublé and Bryan Adams. Allen called his music derivative, Lefebvre tells me, while we are driving in his car on a Salt Spring Island road one sunny afternoon. He shares the criticism from the well-known and outspoken music manager without a trace of disappointment. I asked him if perhaps the project was a vanity project and also a convenient escape from his upcoming sentencing. He nodded and agreed that, in part, the project grew out of those things.

A couple of years after the second album, Lefebvre was still out on bail, quietly waiting. The FBI had been busy busting other online gambling executives, and Lefebvre believes they didn't want to finish with him because they were still negotiating plea bargains with others, and those negotiations benefited from nobody knowing his fate. So he kept on in a state of limbo, and music. In February 2011, Lefebvre formed a five-piece band, including his studio players James Hutchinson, Greg Leisz, Patrick Warren and Bill Payne, and drummer Ricky Fataar, also from Bonny Raitt's band. They did a few shows in western Canada, opening for the Don Felder Band. Lefebvre was paying Felder for the privilege of playing, on top of the fees he was paying for a manager, publicists, his band and the roadies. Wearing a rhinestone-studded Cuevas jacket emblazoned with red roses, guitar strapped on, he stepped out on stage to full houses at the soft-seat theatres, and he'd play for around forty-five minutes or so. He sang a song called "Mr. Bully Boy," enunciating every word:

> "Hey Mr. Bully Boy, put me in jail
> Listen to my phone calls and read all my mail
> More guys in stir here than there are in Russia
> Put 'em all away and see how that does ya
> Justice was a word that used to have sense
> Now it's just another barb in your fence
> Land of the Free, incarcerate me."

FIVE

"Charge Me Triple"

JOHN LEFEBVRE DIDN'T just spend money on recording albums, buying sparkly jackets and flying wherever by private jet. He spread the stuff around, to whomever he felt deserved it, whoever asked, or both. He'd leave restaurant tips so outrageous that, several times, servers had followed him down the street shouting, "Sir, I think you made a mistake!" When Lefebvre was going through his third divorce, this time to his Costa Rican wife, Cecilia, he hired his lawyer friend Pat Blocksom to represent him. He instructed her, "Charge me triple." Blocksom, who already made a nice income as a family lawyer, scoffed at the suggestion. "Why would I do that?" she said. Lefebvre doesn't remember that particular episode, but he does recall telling an interior designer in Los Angeles to also charge him triple.

The interior designer had offered him a discount, and he thought that was silly. "When they'd try to offer me a discount, I'd say, 'Nah, I'm a full-price guy. In fact, charge me triple instead.' I remember saying, 'Why should I be the only rich guy?'" Unlike Blocksom, the interior designer accepted the generosity.

His friend Geoff Savage, who was his long-suffering financial adviser for several years, listens to this story and interjects: "And so he ended up paying $20,000 just to have a piano moved into his house."

"I don't have the vaguest recollection of that," Lefebvre responds. "But if I did do that, I bet it saved me a lot of trouble. The piano was $85,000 and the staircase was round, with walls."

We are seated on the patio of Lefebvre's oceanfront island home, surrounded by trees and cobalt sky overhead, the ocean calm and glinting. It is the dead quiet of summer, and Lefebvre spends most of his time on the island or at an apartment he and Hilary own in Vancouver. The apartment also looks over the ocean. Life is quiet these days, but he can't complain. If he weren't banned from the U.S. for his status as a felon, he'd spend time in New York, but as it is, Hilary goes without him. Lefebvre has recently applied for a waiver on his criminal record so that he too can enter the U.S. It's become important that he is free to travel, as part of his next life chapter, the one where he becomes a speaker on the lecture circuit, whatever that looks like. Hilary, who has delicate features and long dark hair, and wears loose fitting clothes over her slender frame, listens to the banter between her husband and his old friend and neighbour. Savage is retired now, but he spent his career in law helping bankers through the intricacies of insolvency. He has the brusque but amiable demeanour of a character that Sam Elliott could play. He's wiry like the actor too. Few were better prepared to try to keep Lefebvre on financial course than Savage, but even he couldn't steer Lefebvre away from overspending on absurd expenses like paying white-collar professionals three times their fee. They'd get into big, semi-playful arguments about the spending, and eventually Lefebvre would grow stone-cold and sullen, and tell him to just let it drop.

"But at the same time, he's telling everybody I'm his manager, the guy who's in charge of all of John's money," says Savage, his voice rising. "But he's spending it all. And then he wonders why I'm phoning him up and telling him he's stupid. Maybe he secretly likes abuse."

Savage says he doesn't like to hear it but, at heart, Lefebvre is a salesman. "John is a salesman, and most salesman are susceptible to other salesmen," says Savage, shrugging. "And he really gets pissed off when I say that, but he wants to impart whatever knowledge he has to you, in the most passionate way. So you will believe it—even if it's complete bunkle."

Lefebvre chuckles and changes the subject. He talks instead about the many nights the two had smoked a lot of pot and drank a lot of booze, consuming "unbelievable levels of self-medication." Savage nods slowly in agreement, and you can imagine the two men loudly intoxicated and bantering back and forth, managing to keep it civil in their way. You can also see why Lefebvre would want his old friend to be his manager. He wanted a shrewd businessman to protect him from himself, but he hired a full-time buddy too. "One who would not even slightly shy away from calling it as he saw it," says Lefebvre.

Savage lives up the road from Lefebvre, in a $2-million oceanfront home that Lefebvre purchased and renovated for Savage and his wife. When Savage was working in Calgary as a successful lawyer, Lefebvre asked him to relocate to Salt Spring Island and work for him exclusively. He asked Savage what he'd need in money in order for the move to make sense, and they worked out a deal whereby Savage would get his standard income, "a wheelbarrow full" of Neteller shares, and use of the house as long as he needed it, even into his retirement years. In legal terms, it's called a life estate. Savage has a grown daughter who's disabled, and Lefebvre, always good to his friends, purchased her a home in Calgary so she could live independently. Like Jane, Blocksom and others who have worked with Lefebvre, Savage is emotionally invested in seeing his friend make the right choices. It's been years since he worked as Lefebvre's manager, but there's a sharp edge of frustration in Savage's voice as he recounts the money lost.

The conversation rolls around to the film production company that Lefebvre started with an old Calgary friend named Joe. It had started out as a handshake deal to make a movie based upon the 1953 novel *Savage Night* by noir fiction writer Jim Thompson. Although the friend had no movie experience, Lefebvre thought they had a good enough idea that he could perhaps try out the role of movie producer. Lefebvre kicked in $6 million as part of a formal agreement, and Joe's job was to raise the remainder of the funding, including from a group of Saudi Arabian investors and others who'd cover the production costs of their big-budget film. The production company bought the rights from Thompson's estate for $400,000 U.S. But as time passed, it became clear to Lefebvre and his managers that the film was not any closer to being made, that Joe was living the high life on Lefebvre's money. "He was spending money wildly and basically treating it as his own, shamelessly," says Lefebvre. After a few years of chasing him for answers, Savage and Lefebvre sued Joe, and they got a judgment against him. He filed for bankruptcy and fled the country, apparently with the rights deal. Lefebvre suspects that "whatever money Joe didn't blow, he hid somewhere else." Says Lefebvre, "He's never had the courage to face me since, much less apologize."

"They weren't all scoundrels," adds Savage. "Lots of people made a tremendous difference in lots of lives, and it could have made a tremendous difference in Joe's life if he'd done this properly. But God," he says, "what a waste. John is wildly generous and enthusiastic and has unbounded loyalty despite warnings from whomever. You can end up with a very nasty result, and Joe is a primary example."

His friends believe he had a naïveté that drew the scoundrels to him. Lefebvre prefers to call it trust. Hilary says her husband believed too much in people: "John would always say, 'You can't blame the person who comes to you needing help for what the previous person has done.' And I kept thinking, 'Yes, you can.'"

His friend Pat Blocksom says Lefebvre got badly burned by many people, and he might have needed that. "People take advantage of you because of your money, and there were a lot of lessons learned for John in all of that," she says. "Lots of lessons about what is important, and being able to toss a bunch of money around doesn't mean as much as having people you can trust, doesn't mean as much as who your friends are."

"It took me a long time to develop healthy skepticism, about seventy years," says Lefebvre, who is sixty-eight years old.

A lot of wealthy people perceive their wealth as something resulting from hard work, sacrifice and determination, and so they see their money as an achievement to be protected. Perhaps because he stumbled into it and never really coveted it, Lefebvre didn't care about hiding it away. He also had a lot of disdain for the way rich people behaved, "considering themselves superior to others and insulating themselves from the world in their country clubs and penthouses, behind their velvet ropes." Lefebvre falls into the self-made millionaire category, which contrary to popular belief, is how the vast majority of millionaires become millionaires. Only something like 20 per cent of millionaires inherit their money (according to *The Millionaire Next Door* by Thomas J. Stanley), and it's been well documented that the family wealth is usually lost by the second or third generation. The first generation was scrappy enough to make the fortune. The second generation saw their parents work hard, so they are more inclined to protect it while enjoying it. But because the third generation never witnessed that hard work, they go on to fritter it away. Self-made millionaires build their wealth, and so they're not about to part with it easily. Obviously, there are exceptions such as Lefebvre, who says, "I guess that makes me a precocious millionaire. I got rid of it when the money was still young."

Lefebvre was a smart young guy, but not the precocious youth who had such an inquisitive nature that he'd spend endless hours after school writing computer code at a time when few even knew what it was, like the legendary Bill Gates. By his teen years, Lefebvre was the prototype slacker, twenty years before "slacker" was revived as popular term, the kid who just wanted to get the girls to like him, and to get high. "I don't remember him working much," says brother Ted.

Lefebvre's adventures with LSD went beyond a few weekend dalliances with friends. His acid dropping became an experiment into opening other parts of the brain in pursuit of true consciousness, an awakening that would surpass the mundane nature of workaday life, that would imbue it all with a sparkly dust of deeper meaning. He still riffs on the concept of mind expansion as if it's 1965 and we are sitting at a be-in listening to Maharishi Mahesh Yogi: "When we were kids, we were taught that God made man. But I love the Jesus quote in the Gospel of Thomas when Jesus says, 'If the flesh came into being because of spirit, that is a marvel. But if spirit came into being because of the body, that is a marvel of marvels. Yet I marvel at how this great wealth has come to dwell in this poverty.' So our species grew into consciousness, and that consciousness into which we grew was absolutely the marvel of all marvels. Not God made the meek, but meek made God. That's some crazy shit, man, not the kind of thinking we were brought up on. You don't build hierarchical Churches on that stuff. What would you ever need a priest for? No wonder the Church never sanctioned the Gospel of Thomas." The new world order has little patience for such considerations, dismissing them as hippie platitudes, particularly youth who've come to believe that technology, not drugs, nor music, is the new democratizing playing field through which we express ourselves and demand justice. Amid the online tech movers and shakers, he must have seemed like a man living conspicuously outside his own time—an anachronism even in the early days of the tech boom, when the tech-bro culture hadn't yet fully emerged as a subculture of its own.

He is about as non-representative of tech culture as a person can get, but he enjoyed aspects of the tech-bro scene, such as the casual work-play dynamism that is necessary to keep the workers immersed beyond average work shifts. He quite obviously enjoyed the absurd amounts of money that is funnelled to those who create successful electronic platforms. But tech culture is decidedly homogeneous, and not just because its members are mostly white dudes: it's about banding together with common ideals rather than standing apart and complaining about the system in which you operate. To fight the system would be to thwart your own privilege. As a hippie holdover that truly believed his generation was creating a new and improved anti-materialist social construct, Lefebvre mostly seems uneasy about his late-in-life privilege. That said, in certain moments, he can seem empowered by it too.

IN THE NEW gilded tech age of wealth, it's accepted that those who have made it big have earned the right to tell the rest of us how to live. While the rest of us have barely noticed the paradigm shift, it's become accepted that the über-rich have also become our new moral compass. Anand Giridharadas, author of *Winners Take All: The Elite Charade of Changing the World*, writes and often speaks about the current mission of the very wealthy to dominate the discourse with messages of do-gooderism as their salve for the central role they've played in creating "the new gilded age." As a few get unfathomably wealthy off new technology, for example, the majority of people are still seeing few benefits from all their breakthroughs. These elite tech billionaires often talk about a new world order where everyone has access, where technology opens doors to opportunities. But there's a price that they don't talk about too. To extrapolate on his ideas using the sharing economy examples noted earlier, car service Uber might have created a slew of minimum-wage jobs for the masses, but it's very likely also wreaking havoc for the unionized taxi drivers who once had job protection. Airbnb might have given middle-class homeowners a revenue stream to pay down their mortgages, but there are clear signs in places like San Francisco and Venice, Italy, that it's also dismantling communities as renters are pushed from their homes. Perhaps the billionaires who got rich from platforms should address the problems they've created? Instead, too often the tech billionaires, now self-professed thought leaders, offer facile solutions for problems that are more personal than political, such as how to lean in, or to work more efficiently. It's as if the intention is to distract the masses from the real issues, such as job losses, gentrification and displacement.

Giridharadas introduced his central thesis in a keynote speech he gave at the 2015 Aspen Action Forum, organized by Washington, D.C., think tank the Aspen Institute. The audience was very likely prepared for more of the highly digestible messaging of so many of the thought leaders hired by corporations and sponsored think tanks and non-profits to do such speeches. But Giridharadas delivered instead the type of medicine that is hard to get down. He asked for their forgiveness in advance, warning them that his message would not be easy.

"It falls on us to ask the tough questions... But we here in Aspen are in a bit of a tight spot," he began. "Our deliberations about what to do about the extreme winning and the extreme losing are sponsored by the extreme winners," he said. The Aspen community reflects the consensus of a mindset that is typical of a worldwide and dominant ethic, and it goes like this: "The winners of our age must be challenged to do more good. But never, ever tell them to do less harm," said Giridharadas in his now-famous speech. "The consensus holds that capitalism's rough edges must be sanded and its surplus fruit shared, but the underlying system must never be questioned." Today's winners have greatly benefited from a reconcentration of global wealth, and they've fought for policies, such as tax shelters, that enabled them to do so.

To avoid those difficult questions of why the system is maintained as it is, the winners elaborate on the need to give back to the losers. Within the consensus, generosity is a replacement for justice. Instead of examining a system in which bad things are happening, simply focus on charitable good deeds. In his book, Giridharadas devotes a chapter to thought leaders, those stalwarts of the TED Talk age who are so favoured by the winners of the gilded age that they are paid tens of thousands of dollars, or even well over $100,000, to deliver speeches. Their messages are simple ones, delivered in a well-rehearsed formula that has the effect of a sugary drink on a toddler, perking up their audiences for the short term but leaving nothing much to ruminate on long term. He cites the case of Amy Cuddy, a social psychology professor at Harvard who rose to thought leader superstardom after she gave a TED Talk on the "power pose," based on her 2010 study showing that if a person spent a few minutes in a "high power pose," like, say, Superwoman's hands-on-hips, legs-wide stance, they could create higher levels of testosterone and lower levels of cortisol. Her TED Talk audience went wild and, of course, she turned the talk into a bestselling book. For those in search of a quick life "hack" to chase away the boogeymen insecurities that haunted them, this was a no brainer. Cuddy's work was later discredited, but Giridharadas cites it as an example of a respected academic who'd gone for the easy route when transformed into thought leader guru. Thought leaders, says Giridharadas, generally follow a three-step routine: focus on the victim, not the perpetrator; personalize the political and zoom inward at the personal level to find the source of the problem; and third, be constructively actionable. Nobody wants to read about how things suck. They want to learn what they can do to fix it, and the sooner the better.

Is Lefebvre a rich guy who wants to offer an easy fix? Giridharadas often criticizes the hypocrisy of the wealthy for talking a good game about helping the less fortunate but then not paying their fair share of taxes. "The rich didn't get suddenly better at algebra . . . ," he told the Aspen crowd, "the rich fought for policies that helped them stack up, protect and bequeath the money: resisting taxes on inheritances and financial transactions, fighting for carried interests to be taxed differently from income, insisting on a sacred right to conceal money in trusts, shell companies and weird islands. This hoarding does not merely correlate with the have-nots' struggles . . . That is the money that would be going to schools, to vocational training, to infrastructure building, to social insurance, to financial aid." Lefebvre's former company had relocated to the Isle of Man partly because it was a tax haven. Instead of giving out $1,000 tips and telling interior designers to charge him triple, wouldn't it have done society more good if he'd encouraged his own company to pay taxes that go to universal health care and education? Lefebvre's response is that the laws allow and even encourage tax avoidance, so the onus of responsibility for those lost dollars falls on the government and its laws, and voters.

He also echoes the oft-heard refrain that he was beholden to shareholders. "One of the things we are permitted to do in a Western constitutional democracy is organize our affairs to our best tax advantage. We don't consider that tax evasion; it's tax avoidance, and we are entitled to do that. There was no rule about our moving our corporation to a tax-friendly zone, or a gambling-friendly zone. And once your company is public, you don't have a choice; you have to make legal choices that accord best with your shareholders' interests. Until we impose regulations on corporations that require them to behave in more responsible, more humane ways, corporations have a responsibility to do everything that is not illegal to further their interests and alleviate their tax burden. Corporations have a legal duty to live up to the absolute minimum required of a good person in our society. They have a duty to pay the absolute minimum in taxes and volunteer only the absolute minimum of other non-profitable expenditures. Charities are given as much in donation as it makes tax sense to give, and no more."

He acknowledges that the same corporations enjoying the tax benefits also hire lobbyists who influence a lot of the government policies around taxation. "This has resulted in

a society that alleviates the burden of the wealthy and over-
looks the usually insurmountable plight of the less fortunate.
I think this is the central problem of our society, and I have
always said that in these circumstances, the money would
be much better spent in my hands than in governments'
hands. I avoided income tax, but in turn I donated $50 or
$60 million, about 50 per cent of the cash I ever pulled off
the table, not including the few thousand dollars I'd hand
out as gifts from my pocket. If everybody who had wealth
fall into their lap—and make no mistake, it does just fall
into their lap, you can't earn $300 million—if they gave it
away like I did, we would have a lot less disparity, the utterly
wealthy would become the *fairly* wealthy, and I would have
no more problem on that score."

But he says that the average person whose portfolio is
invested in unethical funds needs to take a look inward too.
He argues that the corruption is widespread and the uncom-
fortable truth is that most of us are playing a part, either
actively or passively enjoying the profits of a corrupt system.
"All the little joe shareholders who are relying on corporate
profits for retirement, and all those corporations making
money and paying the absolute minimum are operating in
a context that is dissociated from traditional concepts of
being 'a good person.' Good cowboys used to look out for the
little guy. Corporate tax and other regulatory regimes have
been massaged by the wealthy to minimize social responsibility and maximize positive revenue.

"The people responsible for keeping it from corruption would rather go mountain biking than fulfill their

civic responsibility by voting. Or they would rather vote for the company that lets their shareholders dump fossil-fuel effluent and tailings into clean rivers. Ask the people in Alberta why they don't regulate the oil industry and they say, 'Because my income depends on it.' Our whole economy is a corrupt one because corporations need to be regulated, and we decline that responsibility. Look in the mirror, because that's where the problem is. Capitalism is not the problem—it is a super-efficient wealth developer. Now, *unregulated* capitalism—that is the problem. And it is caused as much by the 'I don't do politics' crowd as it is by the 'fiscal conservatives.'"

Lefebvre is for taxing wealthy people, such as the scheme proposed by U.S. senator Elizabeth Warren, for a while one of the Democratic presidential candidates for the 2020 election. Her proposed wealth tax would apply to fortunes higher than $50 million, at which point the rich person would be charged a 2 per cent annual rate on their entire wealth. For those worth in excess of $1 billion, there would be a surtax of 1 per cent per year. Economists have calculated that the tax would raise $2.75 trillion in revenue over a decade. Critics say it has several flaws.

However, it's a popular proposal, since it would affect only the wealthiest 0.06 per cent of Americans. Lefebvre embraces the idea. "If they could do that in America, that would assure day care, health care and post-secondary education for everybody without a pay wall, and there would still be $1 trillion left over. It is wealthy people's responsibility to pay their fair share. No one should be able to hide behind income tax rules made by the privileged for the privileged."

People argue against Warren's idea because they say that rich people will just find a way around it and cheat the system. But there are some welfare recipients who cheat the system too, Lefebvre says. "And that doesn't mean you cancel all welfare payments."

AS A RESULT OF HIS upbringing, Lefebvre's generous community splurges often favoured single moms as the benefactors. The newly rich Lefebvre was always giving single moms on Salt Spring Island a couple of thousand dollars to help with the next month's rent, usually without any warning. Others wanted to start a business, or launch a website, and he'd give them a few grand. One time, his regular server in a restaurant told him she was going to Los Angeles to meet with friends for Canadian Thanksgiving. Lefebvre happened to be going to his Malibu house for Thanksgiving as well, so she invited him to her friends' house for a turkey dinner. He went over, had dinner, and listened as she explained how she was having difficulty getting an album recorded. She thought her investor was being too controlling. A conspicuously extravagant Lefebvre said, "Fuck that, here's $30,000" and wrote her a cheque that night. "She blanched," he recalls. "She was kind of nonplussed." He also offered the rest of the group to fly back home with him on his private jet. "They didn't know the vastness of my wealth. Not many people did, really." But they eventually learned, because on the island he had earned the nickname "Mister 100 per cent" because of his habit of tipping 100 per cent on his restaurant bills. As for the young woman with the album, she took his money and made her record, but then set aside her recording career. Instead, she returned to Salt Spring and became a stay-at-home mom and entrepreneur. Lefebvre later found out that she wasn't a starving artist at all but came from a pretty well-off family. He shrugs. Sometimes he'd take into consideration whether the person he was financing had actual talent, or if giving them money would make the world a better place. By way of example, one friend from his law-school days in Calgary, Murray Pettem, coached ringette—a Canadian hockey-type women's sport involving an ice rink, hockey skates, a stick and a plastic ring. Pettem helped run a ringette league in Calgary, coached teams and worked hard as a lawyer helping low-income people, so Lefebvre surprised him with $1 million. "I just knew that if Murray had more time on his hands, the world would be a better place."

Lefebvre never cared if he heard from the recipients of his donations ever again. He didn't care if they followed up on what they did with the money, or if it changed their lives for the better. He gave them money and wished them well. Some kept in touch, like his cellmate in the Manhattan jail. The man was living in a tough neighbourhood in the south Bronx, and when he got out of prison, Lefebvre gifted him a total of $20,000 in about a dozen instalments, to get a leg up in life. Lefebvre later noticed photos the man shared of himself on Facebook, wearing expensive hip hop haute couture. He might not have spent it all wisely, but Lefebvre believes he would have learned something valuable. "There is no better lesson about money than learning how easy it is to blow through a small chunk of it." Lefebvre feels good about the majority of people he gave money to, and he says they deserved every penny and then some. But there were the ones who kept coming back for more money, who started to depend on a handout. Lefebvre had to manage those ones, he says. "I have a bit of a formula that I go through when that happens. If they are people who are casting about for ways to help fulfill the responsibility of helping their children, I would be apt to help them a bit, but I'll tell them that they can't rely on me this way for much longer. Others would come back and ask me for more and more, so they didn't have to get another job. Then I'd say, 'Sorry, I have been as generous with you as I can. There are others in deeper shit, so I have to say no, because I don't have as much money as I used to.'"

He gave a couple of million dollars to a group of people who wanted to turn a pond full of algae into biofuel. Their intentions were likely sincere. Algal biofuel held a lot of promise and had even inspired major fossil-fuel companies to do extensive research until the idea was abandoned because it would take too long to deliver results. Only a few algal biofuel enterprises continue. "Yeah, I wish I had managed it better, but the mistakes I made weren't philanthropic. The mistakes I made were bad investments, thoughtless investments, just throwing money around," he says.

Successful businesspeople often have an astonishing ability to memorize and recite numbers, and are generally pretty good at on-the-spot calculations. They absorb numbers because they live in a world ruled by numbers, whether it's the price per square foot, or per door, or the median price or total sales or inventory decreasing or rising, or year-over-year averages. Lefebvre isn't hung up on numbers, as in how much his assets are worth, or what he's given away. He's spent millions of dollars on projects that never materialized, says Savage. "What we love about him is what is ultimately very difficult to deal with. What you love is what you hate. And you really hate it when it's your job to rein it in," says Savage. "The enthusiasm and passion and emotion is what we love about John, but it's impossible to manage him. When I came out here, I was trying to tell him what to do—or what not to do, primarily.

"When standing on the sidelines, watching him, it's all very wonderful. And he likes cheerleaders, for sure. But I was the anti-Christ trying to rein in the enthusiasm, and it's very difficult to do. He attaches to people. He meets somebody and develops an emotional attachment to them or possibilities for them and wants to trust them. Compassion and empathy are the end of him," he says, laughing. "No, not really," he adds. "But sometimes it doesn't pay off."

In his defence, Lefebvre responds: "I've wasted probably $10 million on stupid investments, and it's just because at the time it didn't matter. It's nothing to waste $10 million when your paper value is $350 million." His friends, however, would argue that the amount he spent on bad investments is actually much higher. According to a *Market Insights* report by Chicago-based Spectrem Group, there are over 11 million people with a net worth of $1 million in the U.S. alone, as of 2018, and it's a growing segment of the population. About 250,000 people became millionaires from 2017 to 2018, and that wealth did not include the value of their primary residence. The very-high-net-worth individual, with a net worth of between $5 million and $30 million, grew to 1.397 million households. The total number of households considered wealthy in the U.S. had nearly doubled since the beginning of the global financial crisis of 2008, according to Spectrem Group president George H. Walper Jr. The bulk of that wealth growth is from making wise investments and diversifying, but there's also a mindset when it comes to money.

American author Tom Corley has made a career out of studying the habits of rich people—those who stay rich and those who don't. "It's one thing to become wealthy. It's another thing to keep and grow the wealth you've accumulated," writes Corley on his Rich Habits blog. He's studied habits of the people who stay rich and those who lose their money. People who keep their money have habits that include reading educational books for at least thirty minutes a day, and they are frugal with their purchases, buying high-end clothes on consignment and then having them tailored, for example. At the other end of the spectrum, a money-losing habit is "want spending," which is when you spend your wealth on immediate gratification, living in the now instead of carefully deciding the things you need. People who update their cell phone with every new version fall into this "want spending" category because they are only buying for reasons of status and the novelty of the new.

Corley refers to another self-defeating behaviour as "supersizing your life," which is when a person gets a sudden increase in wealth and responds with major expenditures. Just because you can buy something doesn't mean you should. It's similar to "lifestyle creep," when a person's income rises and their spending incrementally rises as well, without them even realizing it. It's similar to the phenomenon of "induced demand," a term used by transportation experts to describe what happens when government responds to congestion by building more freeway and highway lanes. Instead of reducing congestion, the new lanes soon just fill up with more drivers. Similarly, a person can succeed at increasing his or her income but then cancel out all that extra money with extra spending. Instead of creating a surplus of cash, they have induced a bigger spending habit: they've filled up the new lanes with more cars. Corley recommends that every person, including the very wealthy, save 20 per cent of their income each year. "This acts as a buffer, preventing you from spending too much and keeping you on track with growing your wealth."

The thing about giving money away is that you want to be respected for your goodwill. It might seem weirdly disproportionate, but Lefebvre has a bigger regret than the $6 million he blew on the failed movie production venture with Joe. He has more regret over the $30,000 he loaned to a fiction writer also living on Salt Spring Island. The man approached him through Facebook, says Lefebvre, and asked him if he knew anyone who could loan money to a writer who had prospects but was in a tight spot. He promised to pay Lefebvre back in six weeks, "three months, tops," and so they met and Lefebvre wrote him a cheque for $30,000. The writer would have heard about Lefebvre's generosity through other islanders. Friends and family agree that, for a time, there were a lot of people on Salt Spring circling around Lefebvre for a handout. Later, he would stop going to the Saturday public market held in the summer because he'd grown so weary of being asked for money.

But in this particular case, the man asked for a loan and Lefebvre agreed. Lefebvre's quasi-money manager Savage drew up an agreement to the effect that the $30,000 was to be paid in one year. That agreement was three years ago as of this writing and the writer still hasn't repaid any of it. Instead, he's given Lefebvre a steady stream of excuses about book payments not coming through, a lack of regular income and illness, and being at the mercy of a producer who made an offer to option his book but hadn't paid, and the tax authorities, and lots of apologizes and sincerely good intentions, and "had I have known" type comments, et cetera, et cetera.

That kind of stuff grates on Lefebvre, because his goodwill toward the stranger wasn't reciprocated. As well, he knows the money could have gone to a truly worthwhile cause. After his arrest, his net worth fell by around 90 per cent, and he had no choice but to choose his beneficiaries more wisely. He knows now that in the past his generosity was exploited, and that he wasn't guarded enough. "I imagined that I could be an example of generosity and non-attachment, and let the chips fall where they may," he says. "I eventually preferred being able to help people out who deserved it, more than just throwing the money around. A couple of those transactions I regretted, but only because the people who got them turned out to be selfish and entitled. I prefer heartfelt gratitude."

Salt Spring Island resident Heather McDonnell, who's worked with Lefebvre on one of his many charitable causes (more on that later), says she hopes he looks back at the good his money did and tunes out those that didn't appreciate it. "It is a small community, and a lot of it is of a good nature, we need support for this and that. But I've worked for successful people, and I've watched them all get to a point where they had to sit down and say, 'What do I specifically want to give to? What's important to my family and me?' They have to narrow it down to cut out the noise of all the people asking for money. I would hazard a guess that John ran into the same issue. It could have been a bit of naïveté on his part as well."

Lefebvre did try to formally organize his giving under the umbrella of a foundation for charitable good works, but he just couldn't turn control of it over to the long-time trusted friends—all experienced professionals—he'd appointed as trustees. He chose a team of Calgary lawyer friends who had known him for decades, socially conscious types who were to act as trustees for the Lefebvre Charitable Foundation. Jane McMullen, Murray Pettem and Michael Greene were each paid $50,000 a year for the job, says Jane, but of course they weren't doing it for the money. Jane was excited that she could take the $14 million or so of foundation money and grow it for various good works that she'd discussed with Lefebvre and the other trustees. "I thought he respected my financial acumen and organizational skills, so I agreed," Jane says.

However, it soon became clear that he had his own master plan, one he hadn't asked for input on from his trustees. Savage puts it this way: "John wanted cheerleaders, but he hired three people who weren't cheerleaders to advise him. That was his biggest mistake. So three really cheap conservative people were hired to help him manage his affairs, and he is unmanageable." Jane recalls attending a dinner party for the David Suzuki Foundation in Vancouver. Suzuki made a speech in which he thanked the Lefebvre Charitable Foundation for its extremely generous $10 million donation—at the time, the biggest private donation in Canadian history (he would later have to reduce the amount when the American justice system dipped into his pockets). Jane was flabbergasted. "That's when the three of us first heard about it. And we were the foundation trustees. That's how John operates. He's a little anti-establishment, and that 'establishment' includes anybody he has hired to try to manage him. You think you've been hired to do a job that makes sense. We thought that we knew what our roles would be, but that wasn't how it worked out. And John knew he wasn't particularly good with money." Not long after, the trustees quit.

The duality of Lefebvre's personality is that he is, on the one hand, a generous softie, and on the other, he gets resentful when people try to tell him what to do. "I think there was some frustration that he felt that I was managing him too much and trying to control his finances, which I saw as my role," says Jane. "In his mind it was 'Just do what I say.'"

While he might have finally learned that merely giving out money doesn't always result in useful outcomes, there remains the question of what he wants to achieve at this juncture in his life. For his 2019 New Year's resolution, he spent $70,000 on the making of a video that involved a videographer and her team staying at his house for four days. The video, written by Lefebvre, shows him talking about his jail-time experience and his moral awakening while visuals of Salt Spring, his Alfa Romeo, and his friends at his sumptuous West Coast home are juxtaposed with images of poor children in Africa.

He tells viewers: "Before my arrest, I was living the wildest trip, with a net worth of hundreds of millions, and definitely living like it. Taking my nieces on a $40,000 spree on Rodeo Drive was just another typical afternoon. Flying my jet from Burbank to Santa Monica to avoid traffic? You bet. That was the new normal. I could buy

anything. I felt like I could do anything. I was invincible.
But the moment those cuffs went on, that feeling evaporated." He says he has come to realize, either because of his
major financial losses or the experimental acid use during
the early years, that he was behaving like another spoiled,
petulant, self-centred prick: "We are not enriched by the
money we take but by the friends we make and keep. We are
enriched by what we give." He suggests we learn with each
other and respect each other, including those from all walks
of life, and he intends to make the spreading of that message his enduring mission in the last part of his life. "It could
be the greatest New Year's resolution in human history," he
says before rising from his chair, allowing the import of that
statement to hang in the air, the equivalent of a mike drop.

Although the video has only had a few views on YouTube,
it's a step forward in his new mission to become a slayer
of dickish behaviours the world over—battling for bigger
taxation of the über-wealthy, for universal health care and
education, and for the end to injustices like clitoridectomies
of girls, not only in parts of Asia, the Middle East and Africa
but in the U.K. and America too. He also had published a
small hardcover book on his musings, which has the look
and feel of a hymnal, entitled *All's Well: Where Thou Art
Earth and Why*. Dedicated to his mother, it is a challenging
read that covers a lot of ground, including wealth, power,
responsibility and decency, with Robert Crumb–sounding
subheads like "How Shit Works, Man." Lefebvre gave copies of the book to all his family and friends, and he gives it

to acquaintances as if handing out a business card. He has given away about a thousand copies, and it can be read for free on his website.

"It's not exactly selling like hotcakes, but I'm not surprised," says Lefebvre. "It's about a huge, difficult, astonishing topic—the challenges for our species going forward, and the principles we might adopt to do so successfully. I am reminded that James Joyce only sold a thousand copies of *Ulysses* in the first twenty years after its publication."

Lefebvre's midlife journey from uninspired, underemployed lawyer to unfathomably rich, accidental entrepreneur who piggybacked on the spoils of a dot-com money maker has, he says, given him an insight he wants to share with the world. Lefebvre considers himself very lucky—he was born into a family that was comfortably middle class, with a mother whose friends were thoughtful intellectual types who'd gather around the dinner table to drink Scotch and talk about the teachings of Pope John XXIII. He wants to spread the message that rich people have an obligation to give back to those who haven't been as lucky, such as those who didn't have the luck to be born into a family that could give them an education, or the luck to be able-bodied and healthy, or the luck to be supported by parents who nurtured them into confident, self-sufficient people with a sense of agency and purpose. He's on a mission.

SIX

A Real-Life John Tipton

HEATHER MCDONNELL WAS working as a waitress at a Salt Spring Island restaurant when Lefebvre made her an offer that changed her life. It was 2005, two years prior to his arrest, and like McDonnell, he was fairly new to the island. Both are friendly, outgoing people, so they quickly struck up a rapport, and Lefebvre explained to her how he wanted to do something helpful for the single mothers on the island who couldn't afford to go on vacation. He told her about the difficulties he saw for his own single mom when he was a kid, and how he wanted to give back. "He offered me the opportunity to help him bring that to fruition," recalls McDonnell. "And he left it solely up to me to make it happen." With the help of Lefebvre's lawyer friend Geoff Savage, they decided to arrange a trip for several single parents and their kids to Disneyland, all expenses paid, all courtesy of Lefebvre.

McDonnell was hired to find the families, organize the trip and accompany them to ensure everything went smoothly. Nobody was to know the name of the Good Samaritan funding the trip, and McDonnell made sure that she kept Lefebvre's name out of it. She worked with a community services group on the island to ensure that she found families who'd appreciate the offer, and to make sure everything about the trip was transparent. Philanthropy can be a tricky exercise, and it's not always so straightforward. There are liability issues to consider, and people might have understandable reservations accepting a weeklong trip from an anonymous person. The community services office approached families and explained how the offer worked, and those who were interested were eventually put in touch with McDonnell. "John wanted it to feel like the vacation was magically dropping from the sky, and I was the middle person protecting his identity and making this happen for all these families. As far as I understand it, everybody was really keen to participate and take part. Most were single moms, people with many health struggles and crises, which prevented them from working."

It turned out that the trip itself, although exciting, was not the thing that was most profound for the group. The true value of it was in the sharing of such a singular experience, something that has stuck with them to this day. Some twenty people went on the four-day trip, which included safe, central accommodation at Disneyland. A staffer from the community services organization went along because she knew most of the participants, so McDonnell was the only stranger to the group. But she quickly bonded with them. "I remember holding these two little hands on the plane on the way there," she says. "I didn't know these people. It was the first time I met them. These kids had never been on a plane before. We ended up spending a lot of time together as a group down there; it created this real sense of camaraderie. I probably got the most out of it, listening to their stories."

Because she'd seen the impact of such goodwill, she knew from then on that she'd want to give back to her community too. McDonnell had been raised in a family that had always donated to causes, but they were international in scope. She hadn't considered that people within her privileged-looking community were also vulnerable. Now McDonnell is actively involved in causes at her children's elementary school, such as giving Christmas packages to families who might otherwise not have gifts for their kids. She too does it anonymously.

"I had always thought of Salt Spring as an affluent community, and I hadn't recognized the struggles that some of the young families had gone through. It forever changed the scope of my involvement in the community, and my level of giving. It opened up a whole new world for me."

The families made thank-you cards for their mystery benefactor, which McDonnell gave to Lefebvre. But she felt sad for him because he'd missed out on an experience that had personally transformed her. "I told him that he had cheated himself out of the experience of seeing what a magical opportunity it was for them; that never would have happened otherwise."

She believes that the act of generosity triggered an understanding among the whole group that they too could give back, no matter how little money they had. "It's that sense of giving. That's what the trip taught us. It was something that was given with no expectations in return. I think that there's such a freedom in that. And I think that it probably affected all of the adults involved in the situation as well... They saw a desire by a stranger to want to give, and to look out for somebody and allow them this opportunity without any thing attached. It renews a little spark of hope in people, and it had that effect on the kids. We are not all on the level [financially] that John is, but it aided me and hopefully the rest of the group, and taught us that no matter what scale you are able to give on, there is value in it."

It's a simple concept: If people could see the good they could create by helping their neighbours, there'd be far less misery. If you see someone who could use your help, whether it's to shovel a driveway for an elderly person or check on a sick neighbour, the gesture builds something bigger. "It ignited that little bit in me. I hope when he looks back he can focus on all of those people he helped. He got younger people involved, and hopefully that continues. I personally hope volunteerism is ignited within the next generation, and I can see that happening, instead of 'Oh man, we could be making money instead of giving our time away.' You hope people will be not so worried about making money."

Lefebvre's friend Pat Blocksom runs a successful family law practice and does considerable charity work in her spare time. She saw her friend become intoxicated by money, and she saw him do a lot of good with it too. But she's not surprised that the thrill of it was fleeting. The studies on happiness and money are well documented, including 2010 Princeton University research that shows that happiness drops off after annual earnings of a mere $75,000. A more recent study out of Purdue University found that for emotional well-being, as in being happy day to day, an income of between $60,000 to $75,000 is required. The same study found that individual earnings of more than $95,000 a year are correlated with lower satisfaction. At that point, debts can be paid and the basic necessities are met; from then on, it becomes about materialism and keeping up with the latest gadget. The ego kicks in, and letting one's ego take charge never ends well. Cameron Chell knows that experience intimately. He paid the price for chasing money.

The incredible story of Chell, who went from a jet-flying multimillionaire to a drug addict living on the street, is a hard lesson about what happens when having the most money is the end game. Chell is the young entrepreneur that Gord Herman worked with before becoming the chairman of Neteller. "Early in my career, I chased the dollar—it was all about making money," says Chell in a phone call from Venice Beach, California, where he now lives. Chell, who was raised on a farm, made half a billion dollars by the age of twenty-six. Unprepared for such wealth, he lost all of it within a few years.

Chell was also a dot.com multimillionaire. By the time his company, called FutureLink, was worth $3 billion, at the peak of the dot.com era, Chell says he was behaving so badly that the new chairman had no choice but to fire him. "It was crazy, the dot.com time," says Chell. "We got over rewarded for what we had created, and we happened to be at the right place at the right time. The only reason I was able to cash out was because I was such a jerk I got fired from the company.

"I got liquidity at the height of the dot.com. It was the worst and the best that happened to me," says Chell, who was the founder and chief executive officer of FutureLink.

"The first year and a half, I would hop on one of my jets— and that tells you the ridiculousness of the story—and I would disappear for months on end. I'd go to different countries, different cities. Usually I got somewhere and didn't move. I would isolate in some shitty hotel in the seediest part of town and really lock myself in, and get drugs. Everybody has their own way of doing it," he says, referring to addicts. "I'd wake up and I'd be clean for a day, and I would make a bunch of bad decisions. I would spend $5 million here or there." He made a series of business blunders that ended up in lawsuits that he then neglected to address. "I thought it would never end," he says of the money. "At age twenty-eight or twenty-nine, I was at the height, doing $10 million deals, and five or six of them at a time. Multiply that times the liability. I was completely irrational and mentally unfit to be making decisions."

At age thirty-five, he was bankrupt, living on the streets of Vancouver's notorious downtown eastside, a drug addict who'd lost his front teeth and was regularly beaten by thugs. All that mattered to him, he says, was getting high. But underneath that desperation to get high was a flicker of something else: he wanted to survive, and he knew if he kept on the path he was on, he would soon die. Drug dealers were beating him regularly, to the point that he had been hospitalized. They had stolen his Jeep, which had been his one remaining possession. But he still had a spare car key in his pocket, and he happened to see the Jeep on a street. So without thinking, he stole it back, terrified that he was being chased as he drove away. He phoned the former chief financial officer of the company he'd built years ago. The thoughtful man, who'd helped him many times before, wired him only a small amount of gas and food money so he could start the long drive back to Alberta to seek out his brother for help. But the journey was long. Chell had to keep stopping for the next wire transfer to pay for gas, because the man knew that if he gave him too much money, Chell would be tempted to buy drugs instead. Chell knew this too. He finally made it to Alberta, nearly collapsing when he arrived at his brother's house. His brother realized Chell must have been serious about recovery this time, because he had gone ten days without drugs. The climb back was long, but by age forty-two, Chell was in a relationship, with a child on the way. He has returned to the entrepreneurial grindstone, working hard on several new upstart companies. By age forty-nine, he was telling TED Talk audiences about overcoming his ordeal. He even opened for the king of motivational speakers, Tony Robbins.

But Chell says he lives with fear too. His past scares him. Big money scares him. The lure of the ego trip scares him the most. He's fifty now, but he worries that he might give into the external validation again. For him, the crazy wealth was a velvet-walled jail cell. "It's a prison, an absolute prison, because now you are married to your ego. You are totally identified with that. [The money] is the only value you now bring to the conversation. There is nothing greater that can separate you from anyone else," he says. "You don't even know you're lonely because you can be the centre of attention. It's incredibly easy to keep yourself distracted—you have this big life. But really, what I find, what I see and experience with people I work with in that position, is that you tend to see people filing the void. That's the addiction."

He adds: "I'm not judging it, by the way. I hope to be very rich again some day. But I'm not ready for it yet."

Chell explains how money turned him into a man who lived purely through his ego, which is that part in us that yearns to stand out from everybody else, that wants to be special. It is a preoccupation with the self, the thing that constantly puts you in contrast to everyone else, whether it's the image of you in the Lamborghini getting looks of envy or climbing a stage to accept a Pulitzer. Of course, money and fame are the ultimate ego fuel, but so too is the act of doing good work. Because it's a sneaky beast, it takes constant work to check that what you're doing or saying isn't the work of the ego. And it takes a lot of self-awareness to be conscious. To get an idea of how difficult it is to be conscious of how the ego is operating, we can look to the teachings of another

Salt Spring Island resident, bestselling author Eckhart Tolle, who writes and speaks about consciousness, and was an Oprah favourite. He once told Oprah: "The ego has many ideas. It says, 'I want to be a spiritual person. I want to be recognized as a spiritual person. I want to be more spiritual than all these people. I'm definitely more spiritual than you.' So, the ego has all kinds of ideas of what it wants to be, and it might even say, 'Yes, I want to be good,' because it wants to have a better image of itself. But on that level, the essential dysfunction of the ego is still operating. This is why we have the phrase 'The road to hell is paved with good intentions.' Because no matter how good your intentions are, when you're still trapped in the ego, it will always take you into conflict."

Chell's hundreds of millions of dollars did not fill him up, make him feel whole, and neither did all the admiration that came with the money. He's even cautious about the motivational speaking he's done, because he wants to make sure it's not appealing to his ego. At first he told himself he just wanted to share his story, but he knew deep down that was bullshit he was telling himself, he says. But then, after one talk, a man in the audience sent him an email, telling him that he too was an addict and that his life was falling apart, and that he could identify. Every time he speaks, Chell gets that feedback, and now he knows that those people are what drive him. It's not entirely his ego, and that comforts him.

Today, Chell coaches other successful men who have addictions to many things, and not just drugs. They might seek out sex, money, gambling or work, and they too are trying to fill a "big empty hole that they can never fill up."

"It feels so good to be liked by people and admired, because it covers up all my own insecurities. It's what being an addict is about, it's taking something from the outside because you are not satisfied with yourself. That pride for me is so deadly. I try to keep it in front of me, because it shows up every single day. I do know for sure that today it might be some little slip of my ego, or smirk, wanting attention, something like that, but for me, if it goes unchecked, three years from now I'm back on the street."

Chell says that he isn't anywhere close to having the wealth he once had, but he is making a good living to support his family. He is still working with a lot of the same people he did all those years ago on the dot.com wave. They are working on several projects, including building cameras for space stations. He has a knack for creating cool projects and getting them to market, and accessing capital, he says, but he has learned that the only way to succeed in business is to accept that it's a grind. "I am really starting to learn that the value in business isn't the people who make it look easy—but it's the people who do the hard things every single day."

Chell used to think money could solve anything, that it could buy happiness. You just had to hire people and get the resources in place. He doesn't think that way anymore. "I'm not rich enough to give millions away, but if I were, I don't think it would have the same impact as the work I get to do with individuals, on what they are going through, and their families. I'm just an addict sharing with another addict. And that is honestly not something that money could buy.

I always used to think that sort of thing was the biggest bullshit statement, but now I get to see that it really is true every day."

FOR THE FIRST couple of years, Lefebvre's philanthropy was generous but unfocused. For a long time, he would give to anybody who asked, or who just happened to catch his attention. There are countless stories of financial support he gave to artists, charitable organizations and individuals on Salt Spring Island, across Canada and elsewhere. In Costa Rica, he helped fund a soccer team for low-income kids and gave money to a dozen schools to do renovations and install wheelchair ramps. He also sponsored a program that funded kids while they went to school, including onto college, and then into a meaningful career. The man who greatly helped Lefebvre channel his philanthropy into a worthwhile focus was an old acquaintance from his LSD-dropping years, Jim Hoggan. The two collaborated to use Lefebvre's wealth to develop a platform that would shape our collective understanding about the environment and define what we now know as climate change.

Their initial reacquaintance began with Lefebvre's habit of making outrageous offers. They had stayed in touch a bit since those counterculture years in 1960s Calgary—when they were both young law students—but not enough to know much about what the other was doing. Hoggan had moved to Vancouver, where he launched a public relations firm in 1986 and grew it into a thriving business that guided politicians, corporations, charities and public institutions through the obstacle course of public image making. He grew his downtown agency into one of the biggest PR firms in the city and had earned himself a reputation as a top guru in messaging, or crafting the public narrative.

One day, in early 2003, his old friend from Calgary called. "I will give you $1 million if you retire by April," Lefebvre told him. Hoggan guesses that Lefebvre said this because he thought Hoggan was still practising law, and Lefebvre wanted to free him from his imprisonment. But he didn't need freeing. Not only did he not need the money but he wasn't interested in retiring, and he enjoyed the PR work he was doing. He'd also come to a point in his career where he had realized that his profession was doing a disservice to the world at large by perpetuating myths about climate change. He told Lefebvre that if he really wanted to give money to something, a great cause would be the Four Great Rivers Ecological Environment Protection Plan, a conservation effort in eastern Tibet directed by Future Generations' founder Daniel Taylor and the Tibetan Department of Science and Technology. Hoggan had been working with Simon Fraser University chancellor Milton Wong and Member of Parliament Flora MacDonald on the project.

Lefebvre's timing was on the mark. Hoggan had been assessing his lifestyle, including the BMW, the wine cellar and the art collection. He knew that a well-respected environmental activist like David Suzuki wouldn't have considered him an ally. His industry was the "Darth Vader" in Suzuki's world. "I went, 'Oh my God, we PR people are at the centre of this whole climate change denial problem—and you get overwhelmed by the reality of it," Hoggan told me. "You sit in these board meetings and you read these documents and you go, 'These environmentalists aren't as crazy as we thought they were.'

"It became something that really concerned me, and still does. People are confused enough without having PR people confuse them more. There is a big responsibility that the public relations industry has for the way people have been misled about those issues." Lefebvre wanted to help Hoggan realize his mission, so he started supporting the causes that Hoggan supported. A couple of years later, they were on Lefebvre's private jet, flying to Tucson, Arizona, to meet with the Dalai Lama. Hoggan had introduced Lefebvre to the Dalai Lama when the spiritual leader had visited Vancouver, and they had been invited to meet with him again in Tucson. On the plane, Hoggan was reading a book called *Boiling Point* by journalist Ross Gelbspan, and he came across a section about fraudulent scientists who were faking their climate science credentials. Hoggan was incensed at this public deception. He voiced his outrage to Lefebvre, who responded, "Okay, what should we do?" Hoggan had read an article in *Fortune* magazine about the power of blogs, and citizen journalism, and he suggested they start a blog. And so they did, calling it the DeSmogBlog, with the tagline: "Clearing the PR pollution that clouds climate science." Lefebvre put up about $500,000 to fund DeSmogBlog each year for the first five years, during which they hired writers such as Gelbspan and Richard Littlemore. Lefebvre's promise to provide any financial backing needed for lawsuits they might face as they did battle empowered the writers. He also offered a $2,000 bonus to the first person sued by a climate change denier, reasoning that climate deniers were unlikely to sue anyway because they'd then have to submit to cross-examination as to where their funds came from. The stratagem paid off—nobody ever did get sued. That first year, they drew an audience of around 400,000 people, and by the next year, more than one million, and then three million the following year. It grew and grew, it won awards, and Hoggan was soon invited to global-warming conferences around the world. They started a Canadian version, now called The Narwhal, out of Victoria, B.C. Hoggan wrote books, including *Climate Cover-Up*, with Littlemore, and *I'm Right and You're an Idiot*, with Grania Litwin, on the importance of listening to one's adversaries instead of taking a hard line. His new platform made him an influencer on a global stage, and one person's work built on another's. *Time* magazine hailed DeSmogBlog as one of the world's ten best blogs of 2011. "We had a huge reach to millions of people," Hoggan says. "It was a big influence behind the work of *Dark Money* by Jane Mayer and *Merchants of Doubt*, by Erik Conway and Naomi Oreskes. Hoggan says he came to a simple conclusion about the moral and ethical dilemmas that he and his corporate clients faced: "If you want to stop being seen as an SOB, then stop being an SOB. It may seem sensible, but that's not the way some parts of the world work."

All the while, Lefebvre stayed behind the scenes, the quiet millionaire philanthropist who had yet to run afoul of the U.S. Department of Justice. Lefebvre figures he gave a total of about $5 million to DeSmogBlog. He'd also given Hoggan the $1 million he had offered him originally because, in his words, he believed the world was a better place with a guy like Hoggan spending more time serving on the board of the David Suzuki Foundation and running DeSmogBlog. "Jim used this money mostly to sustain his law firm in his now-frequent absence. Then he was hooked, and started spending his own money, again, for the same purpose. People don't typically imagine that generosity and public service are the best things to do with money, but after they get a taste of what that feels like, the rest is history." Lefebvre had found a way to make his money matter, and for it to sustain itself. The men's message about global warming and our complicity as a capitalist society that worships portfolio growth got media attention. The ripple effect that Lefebvre's money saw at a micro level on Salt Spring Island grew to a macro level.

Lefebvre also put hundreds of thousands of dollars into a sustainability research initiative that saw ten thousand people interviewed from 2005 to 2011 on issues of sustainability and environment, which became valuable research for social anthropologists who wanted to develop ways to explain the problem to people.

Hoggan connected Lefebvre's money to other projects, big and small, including the arrival of the Dalai Lama in Vancouver. In 2005, Lefebvre funded the launch of the Dalai Lama Center for Peace and Education, which enabled organizer Victor Chan to bring the Dalai Lama and other Nobel Prize winners to Vancouver for the Vancouver Peace

Summit. The intention of the centre is to create a better learning environment for children based on compassion and community engagement. Chan, who has known the Dalai Lama for decades and has co-written books with him, had proposed the idea to create the centre after the success of the summit, and the Dalai Lama had agreed to it. Chan says that "the Dalai Lama had created quite an impact on the city about the importance of less tangible ways to educate, by focusing on emotions and social intelligence, and what he would call 'education of the heart' that goes outside of the usual parameters of the curriculum, so I said that we had to find a way to continue the momentum."

The always-prudent Geoff Savage would sometimes intervene when Hoggan proposed yet another project in need of Lefebvre's support. "He would say to me, 'Leave John alone; stop bringing these people with their hands out,'" Hoggan says. But there were just so many worthy projects that needed help." And it wasn't the quantity of Lefebvre's donation that had profound effect; what mattered most to his beneficiaries was that he gave at all.

A COUPLE OF cases illustrate the profound effects of Lefebvre's giving. In these instances, his money was connected with relatively small, but tremendously useful, projects elsewhere in the world. These aren't cases of infusions of major cash but rather were proportionally minor donations that, because they were well considered, continue to have a lasting impact on many lives. They demonstrate the enduring power of donations that are channelled deliberately and effectively, versus simply giving money away impetuously, without a plan. The process requires a proper channel through which to donate the money, and people on the ground to ensure its effectiveness. The point is also that it didn't take huge sums to make a difference—quite the opposite.

Let's start with sewage. Efficient sewage is not high on everyone's list of charitable causes. And yet, it's a crucial necessity of everyday human life. Westerners take for granted clean drinking water and sewer systems. But in India, millions and millions of people do not have safe drinking water or access to a sanitary sewage system. Sewage runs in the streets and playgrounds, making kids sick and contaminating drinking water and water used for crops. Dr. Gurdev Gill is one of those people you aspire to be, the sort of person who just doesn't give up as long as he knows there are people suffering. He was a medical graduate from the University of British Columbia, the first doctor of Indian origin to open a private practice in Canada. He founded a non-profit group in 1974 in order to help villages in Punjab, because it greatly troubled Dr. Gill that 800,000 people die each year from simple gastroenteritis—which, in North America, is merely a stomach flu that you recover from in a week or two. In the vast majority of cases, death is preventable.

Dr. Gill, now a retired Vancouver physician, started his registered charity with the injection of $100,000 U.S., supplied by Lefebvre, and he turned it into about $2 million worth of rural project developments, with help from the Punjab government and a lot of resourceful-ness. As a result, hundreds of thousands of people have been provided with basics needed for a good life: clean water, sewage infrastructure, paved roads, solar-powered streetlights and even computers for the local schools.

A big reason for his success lies in something Lefebvre himself is not always capable of: close oversight and detail-oriented project management. In the right hands, his money did enormous good. It literally saved lives. The project also gave jobs to both men and women, who now no longer have to travel outside the village to find work. In a healthy environment, with a normal mortality rate, the people feel empowered—and hopeful. The streets are clean and walk-able. Their lives are enriched because they don't have to worry about basic necessities. They are freer.

And then there is the case of Cuban cows. Wendy Holm changed lives with even less money than Dr. Gill received. A retired agrologist who worked as an agricultural policy con-sultant, she runs volunteer projects in Cuba when she's not at home in British Columbia. In the late 1990s, she had turned her attention to Cuba, where there was an economic down-turn after the fall of the Soviet Union. She met with Cuban officials and raised the idea that their countries could mutu-ally benefit from a sharing of knowledge between Canadian and Cuban farmers. The Cubans were keen. She raised pri-vate funds of $90,000 in six weeks so that twenty-nine Cuban farmers could mutually go to British Columbia for a three-week tour. Over a twenty-year period, a total of some sixty Canadian farmers visited Cuba to check out its farms.

The Canadian farmers were impressed. Cuba had been moving away from a Soviet-style reliance on chemicals and pesticides and was opting instead for biological pest controls and cropping methods. Cuban farming is run by about five thousand cooperatives, and the members are key players in the Cuban system. They have their government's ear. Over coffee one day in downtown Vancouver, Holm told me about grazing methods, a topic that I'd never remotely explored. But her enthusiasm made me grateful that there are people like Holm who care about such things.

It started with a milk shortage. The Cubans were facing a drop in milk production. Long ago, Fidel Castro, ever the micro-manager, had pledged that each child under the age of seven would receive one litre of milk per day. But his goal was not being met. To get more milk to Cuban kids, the group introduced the use of "pedestals" for rotational grazing. Rotational grazing is a grid system divided into quarter acres. The grazing cows move slowly around the grid until they've returned to the original pasture, where the grass has regrown. Pedestals are long rows of legume hedges, from which the cows graze. The result is more surface area of legumes for the cows to munch on, so it's a far more efficient use of space. Holm wanted to help expand the concept in Cuba, so in 2010, with the support of a non-profit, she sought out funding from a government agency that promotes human rights and helps reduce poverty around the world. She was told that the Canadian agency would provide a $75,000 grant toward her project, but with a catch: she had to raise $25,000.

She approached Hoggan, who was a board member for the non-profit, called International Centre for Sustainable Cities. He knew exactly who to call. They flew to Salt Spring Island to present the idea to Lefebvre, and without thinking twice, he gave Holm $13,500 toward the pilot project. Later, once it got going and the year-long government funding ended, he kicked in another $25,000.

Like a lot of experiments, it had its ups and downs. After a few years, the pedestal-grazing model failed. It was too difficult to grow grass between the pedestals. When they switched to a faster growing grass, it grew too high, and the shade caused a fungus to take hold in the legume beds, destroying them. But the project had many successes, such as improved irrigation, better nutrition for calves and improved quality of the milk houses. Holm has no regrets, because the project helped the participating cooperative boost its milk production, which had been the Cuban goal. And she connected farmers in Cuba with farmers in Canada, which likely wouldn't have happened otherwise.

And then there was the mother of all donations. Lefebvre's contribution to the David Suzuki Foundation set a record for the biggest private donation in Canada. He'd originally promised a donation of $10 million, but once the U.S. Department of Justice came after him, he had to reduce it to $6 million. He might have lost the vast majority of his wealth, but he was determined to give the foundation the money he'd committed to. Hilary, who was just getting to know Lefebvre when he was arrested, remembers being struck by his intense concern that he might not meet his promises to fund various charities and people. When Hoggan was a kid, there was a popular fictional TV show called *The Millionaire* about a wealthy man named John Tipton who went around and randomly selected people to give $1 million to. Tipton's identity was never revealed. The show, which ran from 1955 to 1960, explored the impact of the money on the beneficiaries' lives. Hoggan has always thought of Lefebvre as a real-life Tipton. He remembers driving down the coast of California on the way to Malibu with Lefebvre late at night and stopping at a restaurant. Their waitress was very helpful with the wine list and shared with them that she was saving money to go to university. When they were leaving, Lefebvre asked the hostess at the door if the tips went directly to the wait staff. The hostess said yes, they did. Outside the restaurant, Hoggan asked him what his question was all about. It turned out that Lefebvre had left the waitress a $2,000 tip.

"When he had $350 million, he could keep doing that. Two thousand dollars was no skin off his nose—he wouldn't even notice it," says Hoggan. "It was a few cents in his bank account. But when his arrest took most of his money away from him, he had to tighten up and be careful, and not be giving strangers money anymore." Lefebvre's unfair punishment bothered Hoggan. "I wanted the good guy to be rewarded."

SEVEN

Good with Everything

IN 2011, THE Department of Justice decided to wrap up its case against Lefebvre, and he flew to Manhattan to face sentencing. A date was set for October of that year. He'd been out on bail for four and a half years. In preparation, he had to make a list of all the significant gifts and donations he'd ever given. He and his lawyer eventually came up with a list that added up to around $50 million U.S., which was a conservative figure considering Lefebvre couldn't remember all of the giveaways. Aside from the many causes he had supported, he'd given friends, colleagues and family millions of dollars. When he and daughter, Emily, showed up at Jane's door with half a million dollars, the first of two such gifts, Emily remembers her crying before she even opened the envelope. In his sentencing decision, the judge praised his standing as a decent citizen who'd attempted to do the right thing: "It's apparent to me that there's a lot of good that you've done in your life, and I suspect that at bottom you are a good person. And I sincerely believe that you have made real efforts to get past this chapter in your life. You will succeed in that endeavour." He went on to wish Lefebvre and his family his very best. Lefebvre and Lawrence were sentenced separately, and each given forty-five days in prison. At lawyer Vince Marella's request, Lefebvre's sentence was reduced by five days to make up for the time he'd spent in Los Angeles and Oklahoma City. Lefebvre's response to the short sentence was mixed. He knew he was lucky compared with the convicts he'd met when he was first locked up in Los Angeles and then in Oklahoma City. Lefebvre knows those guys would have laughed at a forty-one-day sentence and said something like, "I could do that standing on my head." Still, he admits there was a part of him that had been hoping he wouldn't have to serve any time at all. "My lawyer was definitely trying for nothing, and I entertained the possibility that he might be successful. To that extent, it was a disappointment."

Lefebvre served his time in downtown Manhattan, Lawrence, in Brooklyn, so their paths never crossed. Because his sentence was so short, he was imprisoned in the pretrial centre, where men were held before sentencing. It was a little less daunting than being locked up with men who already knew their fate, but only slightly less miserable. He spent his days trying to block out the cacophony of loud radios and men yelling at each other. He purchased a $35 Sony

Walkman in the commissary and quickly discovered that it was Beethoven month at WQXR, a New York classical radio station. His comforts were reading books, playing chess and listening to sonatas, concertos and symphonies with his headphones, tucked into the most remote spot of the common area that he could find. He enjoyed chatting with his young bunkie Sam, a gangster who wanted to go the straight and narrow once he was released (to this day, he and Sam still message each other on Facebook). Slow as they were, the forty days passed. He had served his time for displeasing the Americans, and he paid a substantial price financially. Lefebvre still owned a lot of shares in Neteller when the FBI showed up at his house that morning. After his and Lawrence's arrests, Neteller stock dropped from about $20 a share to 20 cents, so shareholders took a major hit. As part of the plea bargain, Lefebvre forfeited $40 million U.S. and Lawrence forfeited $60 million.. Their money went to the U.S. government coffers. It was their punishment for daring to facilitate offshore gambling to an American market. The hypocrisy of it stung. Only two years later, in 2013, the state of New Jersey would legalize online casinos, online sports betting and online poker, becoming the largest market in the U.S. for regulated online gambling. Online gamblers can play slot games, poker, blackjack, keno, roulette, craps, Texas Hold 'Em and endless other table games on New Jersey sites. With a couple of dozen legal and licensed online casinos, the market in that state nearly surpassed $300 million for 2018 alone, and it's steadily climbing, according to the website Play USA. You can play on your home computer

or cell phone. The majority of major American casino opera-
tors own a New Jersey–based online casino site, says Play
USA. In May 2019, New Jersey governor Chris Christie
wrote in an opinion piece for the *Detroit News*: "For years,
offshore betting companies have provided for mobile betting with zero transparency and zero tax revenues for states.
If states want to stand a chance at persuading those bettors
and new, prospective bettors to participate in a legal, regulated market, they need to make it as easy as possible."

Online U.S. casinos have earned an estimated $1 bil-
lion since they launched in 2013. States that have legalized
online sports betting and casinos include West Virginia and
Pennsylvania, and Indiana, which allowed sports betting in
2019. The online gambling industry has played a key role
in the economic recovery of Atlantic City, a bricks-and-
mortar gambling destination that had been losing ground
to online players. And the payment transfer process is a
breeze. Online casinos use Visa, MasterCard, PayPal, and
various e-wallet companies with names like PayNearMe,
eCheck, and yes, Neteller. Neteller is now part of U.K. company Paysafe Financial Services. "As one of the world's
largest independent money transfer businesses, we process
billions of dollars' worth of transactions each year," reads
the Neteller website. The service holds uncleared, in-transit
funds in independent accounts—using the same system that
Lefebvre and his team had used.

Once he finished his jail time, Lefebvre was deported
back to his home on Salt Spring Island, where he remains.

These days, he's more sanguine on the subject, and even accepting of it. His more restrained opinion is likely influenced by the fact that he's been allowed back into the U.S., with an entry waiver he received in the fall of 2019. "The injustice I suffered was so minor compared with what so many others have to slog through. I completely accede their right to do what [the U.S. authorities] did. It's almost their responsibility to do that, to make sure people who decide to take the law into their own hands, to make justice decisions for themselves—in other words, criminals—can be managed properly. I think the Americans were enforcing more or less a supportable interpretation of what the law was."

With the exception of Lawrence, who he's remained estranged from, it wasn't lost on the other investor-founders of Neteller that Lefebvre had taken a bullet for them. He hadn't just forfeited $40 million U.S. and spent more than a month in jail, but he had endured nearly five years of stress dealing with the panic of the unknown jail time because of the senior title he'd held. Canada Revenue Agency recently wanted $7 million Canadian from Lefebvre for his Neteller earnings. Lefebvre suggested a "fairness calculation," and his former partners stepped up to help cover the $7 million, which was a gracious and equitable solution. Only Lawrence remained silent, says Lefebvre. When he talks about Lawrence he gets quiet, and looks restrained, as if there are things he'd like to say but he is choosing not to.

It was not long after he gave up the $40 million U.S. to the American government that Lefebvre began turning away people who'd ask him for money, including funding for a project. After the arrest, he'd tell them, "I'm not the man that I used to be." The arrest, he says, gave him the excuse he needed. He'd been asked for money often enough that he'd grown used to it, but having to say no bothered him. Instead of feeling imposed upon, he seems remorseful about having to turn them down, as if he somehow owes them.

When people think about the money he's blown through, they generally have one of two responses: a sort of awe that someone would do that, or annoyance that someone could be so careless. Perhaps the way people react to his attitude about money says more about those people than it does Lefebvre. Perhaps we can't imagine it because we think money makes us better. Why would anyone give that status up? Or perhaps the thought of giving so much away speaks of a deep-seated fear of going broke, of living on the street, of dying poor. Perhaps there is also a sense of schadenfreude that someone could be so foolish as to part with such a substantial sum of money. Perhaps it's unthinkable because of a generational transference of trauma, having heard the stories of parents or grandparents who lived through the Great Depression and were jobless and broke, or endured the Second World War, and food rationing. Often these stories are told in hushed tones of shame, as if there could be nothing worse than poverty. For most people, money is like bubble wrap, a protective layer against reality.

His long-time friend Jane can't forget a particular moment: Lefebvre's reaction when his lawyer Vince Marella had broken the news to him that the U.S. Department of

Justice had frozen all his bank accounts. "There's a chance you'll never see any of your money again," Marella said. Lefebvre put his head between his hands for a moment, sat up straight, took a deep breath, exhaled and said: "Well. It's been one hell of a ride." When she heard this, Jane couldn't believe the response. "I would have completely broken down, but he just took it in stride." All these years later, she still sounds baffled.

If true friends are people who have your back, who look out for you and tell you the truth when you are blowing it, then Lefebvre was blessed with a group of true friends. There were many warnings, many attempted interventions. Jane, intensely practical and responsible, spent a lot of time exasperated and aghast at her friend's attitude toward his future security. "There were times I went to him and said, 'I am not trying to control your life—I am trying to preserve enough money so that when you are an old man, you have enough money to live a comfortable lifestyle. That's what I am trying to do.' And he would say, 'Yeah, I know, but I want you to write a cheque for this anyway.'" If he was addicted in the way of a gambler, his expenditures were worse than gambling, she says, because there was no return. "If you are pushing your chips toward a dealer, at least you might get something back. But that's not what he was doing. Over and over and over he was warned. Eventually I quit, and so did the other trustees, because we couldn't be party to it."

Savage says that when he got really frustrated, he'd try creative interventions. He would compose his friend little GIFs of $100 bills flying away, emailing them to him with the caption: "Hello! Goodbye!" One day, he tallied all the upcoming projects and donations Lefebvre had planned, and calculated a shortfall of about $60 million. "Most of the projects had good possibilities," Savage says. "But sometimes it doesn't pay off."

Lefebvre talks appreciatively of Savage, perhaps more so than of any of his friends.

"He did a lot for me, and he shouldered a lot through a very difficult ten-year management of my career. He watched me blow through my money, and he watched me get arrested, and then he watched me face sentencing and all the rest of that, and he was a nervous nelly and it wore on him a lot." We are talking on the phone, Lefebvre at his home on Salt Spring Island, where he still delights at the sight of sea lions, whales and eagles. It's not unusual for him to stop the conversation to admire something passing by. He admits he was sometimes showing off when he'd throw his money around, proving to the world that he was so unimpressed with his new-found riches that he could just give the stuff away. "Being blasé about it is, among other things, an ego trip," he says. "People quite properly fear doing what I did—very nearly giving it all away. Part of the package of getting wealth is the clutching onto it. But I was solidly convinced from the beginning of the big money rolling in that whatever else happened, wealth was not the most important part of me. I would be okay, mostly because I knew that. "

The plan had always been to give most of it away. He says that the hoarding of wealth and the fear of others taking it from you is counterproductive, because if you share it and make sure others are secure and educated and have dignity and purpose, you don't have to worry that they'll take it from you.

"Billionaire types, corporate billionaires, they hoard capital to themselves when they could be developing much more capacity in their customers. The more money that goes around, the more money that comes around. We have to start thinking differently about it, because the amount of wealth in the world has vastly exploded. Wealth is probably infinite, and the way for people to get richer isn't to hoard but to make sure everybody is as productive as they can be, creating more and more wealth. A rising tide lifts all boats, and more importantly, it makes rickety boats more sound, more useful and more productive."

Or, put another way, once you help people, you no longer have to be responsible for them: "People don't need your money anymore because they can make their own. Plus, people who you help don't bust your balls."

Lefebvre is frank about his finances. His investments were earning him around $200,000 a year, he figures, but some were unsuccessful, and his dividends have continued heading south. In the last five years alone, he says he's gone through about $2.5 million on operating Stonehouse and maintaining a couple of other properties. Because they are expensive assets to hold, he is looking to unload his real estate holdings, except for his primary residence. And yes, there have also been some giveaways in the last couple of years, to those who need it. "Here I am, with a bit of really nice real estate, and that's about it—but it's still a lot more than 99 per cent of people on earth have."

Canada Revenue Agency is after him for up to $1 million in personal taxes. There's also that. But he says his lawyers insist he owes none of it. Lefebvre hopes the agency will be merciful, though he knows too that he might be overestimating a bureaucracy. It may be a major hit, but one he's prepared to take: "I'm honoured to pay taxes in Canada. We just have to agree on how much is right. I'd rather deal with the remainder of my money my way." He needs what he's got left because the plan is to keep giving. Once he's sold off enough assets, he can give to various charities on a smaller scale. Also, he wants to revisit those albums he recorded years ago in Los Angeles. There's something in that project that's left him feeling unsatisfied. That's another thing he's got to see through to the end, though what that end looks like remains unclear.

Instead of figuring out what he should do in life, he's always just decided what he *didn't* want to do. Looking back, he thinks he could have had a career in interior design, or communications, if he'd applied himself. "Most of my career choices were utterly expedient. They weren't forward-thinking or about long-term planning." For a man who enjoyed a decade of decadence that few will ever know, he strikes me as someone who's still waiting for something great to happen. His daughter, Emily, tells me that she thinks her father wants to be an influencer, to do good. "He wants people to believe in and enact their democratic rights and responsibilities, and he wants to save the planet from climate change." She says her father has abandoned the idea of fame. "For sure there is a part of him that wanted a bit of recognition or fame for the music, but that's changed." She doesn't plan around an inheritance because for ten years she watched her father "buy another house and sell it at a loss, buy another house and sell it at a loss." And she's okay with that, since her father has already been generous to her. He also paid off her mother's mortgage. Her only regret is that her father gave to people who deceived him, like the pilot who was using her dad's jet to charter it to other people without telling him. Lefebvre had never told me this story, which makes me think there were so many pilot types in his life that he's lost track of them all. Otherwise, she says, "I can't imagine being in his situation and not being the same way."

If the plan was to give most all of it away, David Suzuki wonders how far he will go. Will he be happy only when it's all gone? When I speak to his other friends and former colleagues, they too wonder how far he'll take it.

One of them, who preferred to keep anonymous, wondered if the money intoxicated him, if he became addicted to the feeling of spending it, and even addicted to the high of giving it away. It's a solid theory, and it's easy to understand the dopamine thrill of throwing money around and seeing the faces of astonishment. But you also think about how easy it would have been to just tuck part of the $350 million fortune into something as dull and conservative as a guaranteed investment certificate. He could have lived off the interest, and the Lefebvre Charitable Foundation that he set up could have grown—instead of evaporating, which is what it did after Lefebvre depleted the funds with his compulsive generosity. I began to wonder if Lefebvre might be hiding money somewhere, just to streamline and simplify his life. When I ask him this, he laughs and says, "No. The FBI and Department of Justice thought that too. But what they found was it's all in plain sight. Always has been."

There's a growing movement underway, and you need look no further than Netflix to find it. *Minimalism* is a Netflix documentary about how encumbered we've become with stuff, not just individually but collectively. Joshua Fields Millburn and Ryan Nicodemus, the subjects of the film, have a reported following of more than 20 million people who are reading their books and essays, and listening to their podcast. Increasingly, they point out, in America, the trend has been to buy big houses and fill them with more stuff. We've become addicted to the expectation that stuff will give us happiness, and yet it doesn't, so we keep going back for more. More than ever before, cheap consumer goods are there to fill this need, and yet happiness levels are not rising. The same could be said for Canada. Millburn and Nicodemus have realized that in doing the opposite— living with less—they've found the true ticket to happiness. In the documentary, Millburn, who gave up a lucrative corporate job, lives in an apartment that looks like a monk's sleeping quarters, with bed, chair, table and a few shirts in the closet. There is no TV, no art on the walls. In the shedding of stuff, they've found true freedom, and they are on a mission to spread the gospel. They don't expect others to reduce their possessions to a few things, but they *are* hoping that they'll see that these things are more of a trap than a release. These millennials have tapped into what hippies like Lefebvre embraced fifty years ago. It might have a new name, but the idea is the same: life has more meaning if you don't play the money game.

Bob Edmunds says there's an inner beauty to Lefebvre's story because it shows that he's true to form. Edmunds says he too is a hippie but, unlike Lefebvre, he's not into philanthropy or loaning money. He tried it, but he got burned badly in a real estate deal with a former friend. "I used to think people were great. Now, I think they are fucked until they prove otherwise." But Edmunds says he was also tight with his cash. In their group of seven investor-founders, Edmunds says he was always "the house of sober second thought," the guy who made conservative financial decisions. In Lefebvre's case, the foreshadowing of how extravagant he would be with wealth was there in the early days, the "thumbnail of the bigger story."

"When push comes to shove, he doesn't want to work that hard, or have a house in the suburbs. He says, 'Fuck it, my interest is in music.' And then Neteller comes along, and it's money beyond his wildest dreams. But he still wants to live like a hippie, and that's why he gives the money away, and does the extravagant shows of wealth, just for laughs." He even wonders if a part of Lefebvre wants to return to busking, like in the old days.

"This is a larger 3-D version of what went down before Neteller," Edmunds says of present-day Lefebvre. "It shows a certain strength of character and a commitment to values, right? Because he was the same guy before he had the money." Edmunds has other business ventures. He and Glavine own a hotel in Costa Rica. He is well-off, but he doesn't need much. He likes to think he's also true to form, and his lifestyle is not unlike when he was a kid without money, preferring to go sailing than motor boating because there's no fuel cost. "Even though I could afford anything, I don't want anything," he says.

The whole Neteller story makes him think about the worldview that everything has to keep on expanding outward in order to be considered a success. "I know that's the basis of capitalism, this growth. It's the basis of our financial markets, of everything. It's a mindset to be dealt with, I think, this whole endless growth thing. It's kind of the problem."

When asked if Edmunds might be right, if he's subconsciously seeking a return to his old busking life, Lefebvre doesn't outright deny it. "He is speaking about something that I think actually has some probative value. I am in touch with something that is more important to me than being able to go to Barcelona, and that is the treasure of being at peace in the moment. Bob might have a point. Maybe I will just go busk again."

Lefebvre thinks about the question of wealth, and what it felt like to be worth $350 million U.S. Some would give him an odd smile, in a way he wasn't used to. "I never completely understood it, but I think it was a shit-eating grin. I was surrounded by shit-eating grins for a long time by a lot of people who I thought I knew, but $350 million gets some people off balance. They don't know how to handle it." Then there were the dear friends who would just say, "Oh, fuck off, Lefebvre" when he needed to be told off. "Those are the ones you treasure."

Later, on another phone call, he adds more on the subject of being the rich guy, and how he responded so differently to the money than did his old business partner, Steve Lawrence. The two never did connect again after their arrests. It wasn't the arrests that broke their bond, says Lefebvre, but the money.

"There were certain ways that I was not impressed with, having all that money. I didn't think I was better than when I had been a construction labourer, or taxi driver. I knew that coming into several hundred millions of dollars didn't make what matters that different. It was partly that thinking that encouraged me to go ahead and behave in generous ways, because it made up for being rich. I didn't want to be a person who hoarded that stuff to himself, which was the opposite of Steve."

Back when he was under arrest, an FBI agent named Roy had found him a curiosity, this rich man on the wrong side of the law who was giving his money away. During one of their investigative interviews, Roy asked him, "What are you going to do after this? Would you do it all over again?"

"No fucking way," responded Lefebvre. "Are you kidding? I'm not a business guy. All I ever hoped was to get back to a net worth of zero, and maybe save a hundred thousand. I think I'll just play music."

"What about your partner, Lawrence?" asked Roy.

"Steve? He wants to be a billionaire. He wants to be Warren Buffett."

The agent shook his head. "Some guys want to be Warren Buffett. And some guys want to be Jimmy Buffett."